The Economics of the Public Sector

Introduction to Economics Series

Kenyon A. Knopf, *Editor*

The Economics of the Public Sector

ROBERT H. HAVEMAN

Grinnell College

John Wiley & Sons, Inc.
New York • London • Sydney • Toronto

43247

Library of Congress Catalogue Card Number: 78-111353

SBN 471 36183 6 (cloth); SBN 471 36184 4 (paper)

Printed in the United States of America

10 9 8 7 6 5 4 3 2 1

Introduction to Economics Series

Teachers of introductory economics seem to agree on the impracticality of presenting a comprehensive survey of economics to freshman or sophomores. Many of them believe there is a need for some alternative which provides a solid core of principles while permitting an instructor to introduce a select set of problems and applied ideas. This series attempts to fill that need and also to give the interested layman a set of self-contained books that he can absorb with interest and profit, without assistance.

By offering greater flexibility in the choice of topics for study, these books represent a more realistic and reasonable approach to teaching economics than most of the large, catchall textbooks. With separate volumes and different authors for each topic, the instructor is not as tied to a single track as in the omnibus introductory economics text.

Underlying the series is the pedagogical premise that students should be introduced to economics by learning how economists think about economic problems. Thus the concepts and relationships of elementary economics are presented to the student in conjunction with a few economic problems. An approach of this kind offers a good beginning to the student who intends to move on to advanced work and furnishes a clearer understanding for those whose study of economics is limited to an introductory exposure. Teachers and students alike should find the books helpful and stimulating.

Kenyon A. Knopf, Editor

Preface

In the United States economy, the impact of government on the allocation of resources is pervasive; about 20 percent of the nation's land, labor, and capital produces outputs which are distributed to the people by some form of government. In this volume, we examine the basis for and process of collective choice, emphasizing considerations of efficiency and equity in government decision making. Because collective decisions are ultimately political decisions, study of the choices and choice processes in this huge public sector is true "political economics."

The primary perspective of this volume is that of microeconomic analysis and, therefore, problems of macroeconomic theory and policy are touched on only peripherally. Consequently, the questions posed here pertain to the effect of public policy decisions on the efficiency with which the nation's resources are allocated and the equity with which the costs and gains of these decisions are distributed among the people. Because most of the public decisions that affect the allocation of national resources involve taxing and government spending, much of the text deals with these public finance matters. The theories of fiscal and monetary economics and policy that are concerned with attainment of full employment and price stability are considered beyond the purview of this book. They are, however, discussed in another volume in this series.

Although the public sector in the United States is composed of federal, state, and local governments, the discussion here deals primarily with issues of national policy. It is judged that these issues are of the widest general interest and enter most deeply into the political life of the nation. It should be emphasized, however, that the principles of public choice presented here are fully as applicable to issues of state and local government policy as they are to decisions at the federal level.

I was greatly assisted in the preparation of this volume by the helpful comments and criticisms of Professors Bruce Davie, Martin Garrett, Kenyon Knopf, William Pollak, and Dennis Weidenaar. While I failed to accept all of their (sometimes conflicting) suggestions, I did heed a significant number of them. They are, of course, absolved from the remaining inadequacies.

I also received substantial stimulation from the "public policy economics" atmosphere of the Joint Economic Committee of the Congress, on which staff I served while on leave of absence from Grinnell College during the academic year 1968–1969. The assistance of Anne McAfee in the typing and proofreading of the manuscript is also gratefully acknowledged. Finally, special thanks are due my wife and family who incurred much of the cost necessary to produce this output. They understand that any *ex post* benefit-cost analysis of the decision to undertake this effort is forbidden.

Robert H. Haveman

Contents

PART FOUR

Chapter 6   **The Federal Budget—Its Construction and Structure**   **89**

Chapter 7   **The Federal Tax System—Its Impact on Efficiency, Equity, and Stability**   **112**

Chapter 8   **Public Expenditures—Considerations of Efficiency and Equity**   **140**

PART ONE

1

The Public Sector and the Private

The economy of the United States is an enormously complex organism. In 1969, it produced final goods and services at a rate of over $900 billion per year.[1] This is equal to about $4000 worth of goods and services for every man, woman, and child in this country. Over 80 million people find employment in this system and earn incomes in the form of wages, salaries, rent, interest, and profits paid by nearly 12 million businesses and over 80,000 governmental units.

The process by which the $900 billion of annual gross national product (GNP) gets produced is not an easy one to comprehend. Through transactions numbering in the hundreds of millions each day, huge corporations with billions of dollars of annual sales exchange money for goods (or goods for money) with each other, with small businesses, and with households. Individual laborers sell their "labor power" to the huge corporation, the small business, governments at all levels, and the household in return for wages. Governments buy both goods and labor from both businesses and households and produce "products" (like highways) which provide services for all citizens. Governments raise money

[1] It will be noted that the modifier "final" is attached to the phrase "goods and services." This signifies that only those goods and services which go to the final purchasers are being counted. Goods (such as flour) which are intermediate to the final good (bread) are therefore excluded. This concept of "final goods and services" is called the gross national product (GNP) by the nation's social accountants.

to finance these purchases by both exercising their constitutional power to levy taxes and selling some of the goods they produce (for example, charging tolls for highway services).

It is important to inquire into the full structure and operation of this economic process.[2] In this volume, however, we shall restrict our questions to a limited part of this economic system—the public sector. In this chapter, we shall present a broad description of the relationship between the public and private sectors in the United States economy and view the basic ways in which their functions differ.

A rough indication of the relative sizes of the public and private sectors is obtained by comparing the size of their budgets. Table 1-1 compares the amount spent by governments on the purchase of goods and services with the remainder of the GNP.

Table 1-1. **Public Sector Purchases of Goods and Services and their Relationship to GNP, 1968**

	($ Billion)	Percent of GNP
Public Sector	$197.2	22.9
Private Sector	663.4	77.1
GNP	$860.6	100.0

From this measurement, it is seen that government "produced" nearly $200 billion worth of goods and services for the society in 1968. This represents slightly more than 20 percent of the economy's final production.[3] Stated alternatively, about 20 percent of

[2] This sort of comprehensive inquiry is pursued in *The Market System,* by Robert Haveman and Kenyon Knopf, and in *Case Studies in American Industry,* by Leonard Weiss, both in this series.

[3] Because the production of the public sector is not sold for a price, its value is difficult to estimate. By convention, it has been agreed to value the output of the government by the value of the goods and services which it *purchases.* Hence, the value of the educational services provided by, say, the city of Washington, D.C., is taken to be equal to the *expenses incurred* by the city in providing teachers, books, paper, and buildings. The value of Interstate 80 is assumed to equal the sum of governmental expenditures to construct and maintain the highway. For this reason, public sector spending which is devoted to the purchase of goods and services is pertinent in discussing the relative sizes of the two sectors. It should be noted, however, that govern-

the total input of the nation's resources—its land, labor, and capital—produces outputs which are distributed to the people by some form of government.

Observing government to be so prominent a producer of the nation's final output, we would do well to inquire into the composition of "government output" and to compare it with the structure of private sector output. In Table 1-2, the public sector is divided into two parts—the federal government and a combination of state and local governments. The outputs produced by each level of government are listed, together with the number of dollars spent to produce each type.[4]

Table 1-2 demonstrates a number of interesting things. First, by far the largest government output is that of national defense (or offense, as the case may be). In 1967, over two-fifths of the total output of the public sector, and over 8 percent of GNP, are in this category and all of it is provided by the federal government. The next largest output is education, and nearly all of it is provided by state and local governments. Indeed, these two outputs comprise over 60 percent of the public sector's production. Second, note that the major outputs listed in Table 1-2 tend to be produced by *either* state-local governments or the federal government. Few functions are undertaken by both levels of government in anything like equal amounts. Finally, it is seen that the majority of the nation's public sector output is supplied by the federal government—over 60 percent of the value of publicly produced outputs is generated at the national level.

In attempting to discern the differences between the public and private sectors, it is helpful to compare the kinds of output produced by each. This comparison is possible by relating Tables 1-2 and 1-3. In Table 1-3, the composition of that part of GNP

ment does not, by itself, generate all of this 20 percent of the economy's final output. About one-half of its expenditures are for goods produced by private business. The other one-half are for the purchase of labor (and other factors of production). Hence, the public sector itself generates about 10 percent of the nation's total "value added."

[4] In forming Table 1-2, it was assumed that those state-local expenditures which are directly financed by federal grants represent federal outputs rather than state-local outputs. Thus, the data in the federal government column include the grant-in-aid expenditures of the national government.

Table 1-2. Federal and State-Local Government Expenditures for Real
Program Outputs, 1967 ($ Billions)

Expenditure Category	Federala	State-Localb	Total $ Billions	Total Percent
National defense	72.8	—	72.8	40.6
Space	4.8	—	4.8	2.7
International affairs	.5	—	.5	.3
Agricultural services	.9	.8	1.7	.9
Regulation of commerce	.1	1.3	1.4	.8
General government	2.2	6.4	8.6	4.8
Health and hospitals	3.3	6.3	9.6	5.4
Transportation	5.4	10.3	15.7	8.8
Education	3.4	35.5	38.9	21.7
Natural resources	2.7	2.1	4.8	2.7
Housing	1.2	—	1.2	.7
Public utilities	—	2.6	2.6	1.5
Police and fire protection	.1	6.2	6.3	3.5
Sanitation	—	2.1	2.1	1.2
Other	9.7	−1.7	8.0	4.5
Total	107.1	71.9	179.0	100.0

Source. Calculated from *Survey of Current Business,* July 1968, p. 36.

a Those expenditures for goods and services which imply government production of real output, including trust fund expenditures and grants to
state and local governments. This category excludes transfer payments to
individuals such as public assistance, veterans' benefits, and interest on the
national debt.

b Those expenditures for programs which imply government production of
real output, excluding that portion of expenditure financed by federal grants
and transfer payments.

which is sold by private businesses to private citizens is shown.

While the output distributed by the public sector to citizens
(Table 1-2) is composed of products like education, national defense, police protection, and so on, the outputs distributed to
citizens by the private sector (Table 1-3) are composed of consumption goods (three-fourths of the total) and investment goods
(one-fourth of the total). Consumption goods are commodities
such as food, clothing, autos, theater tickets, and so on. Investment goods are commodities which are added to the nation's
capital stock, such as factories, houses, and machinery.

Another crucial difference between the private sector outputs

Table 1-3. Output Composition of GNP Sold to Private Sector Buyers, 1967

Output	$ (Billions)	Percent of Total
Consumption goods	492.2	80.4
Food, beverages, and tobacco	118.6	19.4
Clothing	50.7	8.3
Personal care	8.5	1.4
Housing	70.9	11.6
Household operation	69.9	11.4
Medical care	34.0	5.6
Personal business	26.7	4.4
Autos and other transportation	63.5	10.4
Recreation	30.6	5.0
Other	18.8	3.1
Investment goods	114.3	18.7
Residences	24.6	4.0
Business structures	27.9	4.6
Producer's equipment	55.7	9.1
Change in inventories	5.6	.9
Net exports	4.8	.8
Total	611.3	100.0

Source. *Survey of Current Business,* July 1968, pp. S-1 and 30.

(consumption and investment goods) and those produced by the public sector is how the goods are distributed to the people. Although almost all of the consumption and investment goods are purchased by people in markets, very few of the public sector outputs are sold for a price. The vast majority of public outputs are provided to members of the society free of charge.

From these comparisons, it is clear why the United States economy is described as a "mixed economic system." The outputs of the economy are neither produced entirely by the public sector (as in a purely socialistic economy) nor are they produced entirely by private business (as in a purely free enterprise economy).

The mixed character of our economy is further demonstrated by the following instances of government and private business activity in particular sectors.

• The total stock of wealth in the form of tangible items is estimated to be about $3 trillion in the United States. Of this total, governments own nearly 20 percent.

• Over 11 million civilians are employed by governments. This is equal to about 15 percent of the employed labor force.

• The United States occupies over 2.3 billion acres of land. Over one-third of this total land area is owned by the federal government. The market value of the government's land, however, is only about 5 percent of the total value of United States land.

• There exist over 280 million kilowatts of electric power generating capacity in this country. Between one-fourth and one-third of it is government-owned. Municipal governments own a substantial proportion of this public sector capacity—over one-third.

• Of the total annual new construction in the United States, about 30 percent is accounted for by public buildings and other structures (such as highways and dams). Of this public construction, however, over 80 percent is performed by private contractors.

• The United States government is a major retailer in the nation through PXs and commissaries. The aggregate sales of these establishments total about $3 billion annually. In terms of sales, the PX (or commissary) as a chain store is larger than either Krogers, J. C. Penney, Montgomery Ward, or Woolworths—each of which is a competitor.

• The federal government accounts for well over 50 percent of the total national expenditure for medical care and health. Indeed, the medical care industry is one of the most heavily federally supported and subsidized industries in the nation.

• A sizable majority—about two-thirds—of total annual research expenditures in the United States are accounted for by the federal government.

While the United States has a mixed economy and while there is wide agreement that it should remain mixed, there exists little consensus on whether the economy should become more public or more private. Many argue that a number of activities now undertaken by governments should revert to the private sector or not be done at all. Others assert that there should be a major reallocation of society's resources from private to public production.

Few, it seems, are pleased with the public-private mixture as it now stands.

To help us understand the ongoing debate about the appropriate size of the two sectors, let us listen to two of the most articulate spokesmen on this question, one on each side of the issue. One is John Kenneth Galbraith, author, Harvard economics professor, and former Ambassador to India, The other is Milton Friedman, University of Chicago economist and prominent critic of the increasing role assigned to the public sector. First, Professor Friedman:[5]

Every act of government intervention limits the area of individual freedom directly and threatens the preservation of freedom indirectly. . . . The widespread use of the market reduces the strain on the social fabric by rendering conformity unnecessary with respect to any activities it encompasses. The wider the range of activities covered by the market, the fewer are the issues on which explicitly political decisions are required and hence on which it is necessary to achieve agreement. In turn, the fewer the issues on which agreement is necessary, the greater is the likelihood of getting agreement while maintaining a free society. . . . A government which maintained law and order, defined property rights, served as a means whereby we could modify property rights and other rules of the economic game, adjudicated disputes about the interpretation of the rules, enforced contracts, promoted competition, provided a monetary framework, engaged in activities to counter technical monopolies and to overcome neighborhood effects widely regarded as sufficiently important to justify government intervention, and which supplemented private charity and the private family in protecting the irresponsible, whether madman or child— such a government would clearly have important functions to perform. The consistent liberal[6] is not an anarchist.

Yet it is also true that such a government would have clearly limited functions and would refrain from a host of activities that are now undertaken by federal and state governments in the United States, and their counterparts in other Western countries. It may help to give a sense of proportion about the role that a liberal would assign government simply to list some activities currently undertaken by government

[5] Milton Friedman, *Capitalism and Freedom* (Chicago: University of Chicago Press, 1962), from chapter 2.
[6] Friedman's definition of a "liberal" should be noted. It is that of 19th century liberalism with emphasis on private property and enterprise.

in the U.S. that cannot, so far as I can see, validly be justified in terms of the principles outlined above:

1. Parity-price-support programs for agriculture.
2. Tariffs on imports or restrictions on exports, such as current oil import quotas, sugar quotas, etc.
3. Government control of output, such as through the farm program or through prorationing of oil as is done by the Texas Railroad Commission.
4. Rent control, such as is still practiced in New York, and more general price and wage controls such as were imposed during and just after World War II.
5. Legal minimum wage rates, or legal maximum prices, such as the legal maximum of zero on the rate of interest that can be paid on demand deposits by commercial banks or the legally fixed maximum rates that can be paid on savings and time deposits.
6. Detailed regulation of industries, such as the regulation of transportation by the Interstate Commerce Commission. . . .
7. A similar example, but one which deserves special mention because of its implicit censorship and violation of free speech, is the control of radio and television by the Federal Communications Commission.
8. Present social security programs, especially the old-age and retirement programs compelling people in effect (a) to spend a specified fraction of their income on the purchase of retirement annuity and (b) to buy the annuity from a publicly operated enterprise.
9. Licensure provisions in various cities and states which restrict particular enterprises or occupations or professions to people who have a license, where the license is more than a receipt for a tax which anyone who wishes to enter the activity may pay.
10. So-called "public-housing" and the host of other subsidy programs directed at fostering residential construction such as FHA and V.A. guarantee of mortgage, and the like.
11. Conscription to man the military services in peacetime. The appropriate free-market arrangement is volunteer military forces; which is to say, hiring men to serve. There is no justification for not paying whatever price is necessary to attract the required number of men. Present arrangements are inequitable and arbitrary, seriously interfere with the freedom of young men to shape their lives, and probably are even more costly than the market alternative. . . .
12. National parks. . . .

13. The legal prohibition on the carrying of mail for profit.
14. Publicly owned and operated toll roads. . . .

The list is far from comprehensive.

The response of Professor Galbraith is equally forthright.[7]

. . . The line which divides our area of wealth from our area of poverty is roughly that which divides privately produced and marketed goods and services from publicly rendered services. Our wealth in the first is not only in startling contrast with the meagerness of the latter, but our wealth in privately produced goods is, to a marked degree, the cause of crisis in the supply of public services. For we have failed to see the importance, indeed the urgent need, of maintaining a balance between the two.

This disparity between our flow of private and public goods and services is no matter of subjective judgment. On the contrary, it is the source of the most extensive comment which only stops short of the direct contrast being made here. In the years following World War II, the papers of any major city—those of New York were an excellent example—told daily of the shortages and shortcomings in the elementary municipal and metropolitan services. The schools were old and overcrowded. The police force was under strength and underpaid. The parks and playgrounds were insufficient. Streets and empty lots were filthy, and the sanitation staff was underequipped and in need of men. Access to the city by those who work there was uncertain and painful and becoming more so. Internal transportation was overcrowded, unhealthful, and dirty. So was the air. Parking on the streets had to be prohibited, and there was no space elsewhere. These deficiencies were not in new and novel services but in the old and established ones. Cities have long swept their streets, helped their people move around, educated them, kept order, and provided horse rails for vehicles which sought to pause. That their residents should have a nontoxic supply of air suggests no revolutionary dalliance with socialism.

The discussion of this public poverty competed, on the whole successfully, with the stories of ever-increasing opulence in privately produced goods. The Gross National Product was rising. So were retail sales. So was personal income. Labor productivity had also advanced. The automobiles that could not be parked were being produced at an expanded rate. The children, though without schools, subject in the playgrounds to the affectionate interest of adults with odd tastes, and

[7] John Kenneth Galbraith, *The Affluent Society* (Boston: Houghton-Mifflin Co., 1958), pp. 251-253.

disposed to increasingly imaginative forms of delinquency, were admirably equipped with television sets. We had difficulty finding storage space for the great surpluses of food despite the national disposition to obesity. Food was grown and packaged under private auspices. The care and refreshment of the mind, in contrast with the stomach, was principally in the public domain. Our colleges and universities were severely overcrowded and underprovided, and the same was true of the mental hospitals.

The contrast was and remains evident not alone to those who read. The family which takes its mauve and cerise, air-conditioned, power-steered, and power-braked automobile out for a tour passes through cities that are badly paved, made hideous by litter, blighted buildings, billboards, and posts for wires that should long since have been put underground. They pass on into a countryside that has been rendered largely invisible by commercial art. (The goods which the latter advertises have an absolute priority in our value system. Such aesthetic considerations as a view of the countryside accordingly come second. On such matters we are consistent.) They picnic on exquisitely packaged food from a portable icebox by a polluted stream and go on to spend the night at a park which is a menace to public health and morals. Just before dozing off on an air mattress, beneath a nylon tent, amid the stench of decaying refuse, they may reflect vaguely on the curious unevenness of their blessings. Is this, indeed, the American genius?[7]

Is there any correct resolution of this debate? Further, are there any principles to which one can look in attempting to frame a reasoned answer? The answer to the first question is *no.* Ultimately, one's view of the proper size of government—of the proper allocation of resources between the public and private sectors—is a matter of taste and personal values. The resolution of the issue will, therefore, be a political resolution, and to that extent one can claim it to be at least politically "correct." That it will also be "correct" from other points of view is unlikely.

The question of whether there exist any basic principles to guide one's answer to the public-private question is a more complex matter. While there is obviously no philosopher's stone, the logic of economics does provide some pertinent concepts and an analytical framework which permit one to reason clearly about the issue and to reach some logical conclusions. At a minimum, this logic enables one to discover the conditions under which markets fail to function effectively. To this extent, it provides some limited guidance—some basic economic principles—in thinking about the need for collective decisions to replace or supplement individual market decisions. And, after all, that is what a judgment on the proper role of government in an enterprise economy is all about. To this and related issues, the remaining chapters in this volume are addressed.

In Part Two, the economic performance of the private sector is evaluated. It is argued that, in most circumstances, the market system operating in the private sector is a highly effective mechanism for getting the right goods and services produced and distributed in an efficient manner. However, we shall point out that there are a number of conditions under which the free market system based on individual decisions fails to operate in the public interest. These conditions induce faulty market signals which, in turn, lead to a misallocation of the nation's resources. When there is market failure, collective action is necessary to correct the misallocation—to get those worthwhile goods and services produced which markets fail to produce. Usually this corrective action is government action.

After arguing that action by the public sector is necessary to correct market failure, we shall, in Part Three, present a simple theoretical framework for judging the economic effectiveness of public sector decisions. This framework is referred to as the *Principle of Maximum Social Gain*. It establishes a criterion for judging the economic worth of a public decision through a comparison of the social costs and gains which it entails. Through this kind of comparison, each public sector decision is confronted by the test, "Is the society better off with the decision than it would be without it?"

In Part Four, we leave the world of concepts and enter the world of facts. There we deal with the budget of the public sector, focusing on the spending and taxing of the federal government. In Chapter 6 we deal with the process of budget making in the federal government and with the structure of both the taxes and spending which compose that budget. In Chapters 7 and 8 the economics of both the federal tax system and the federal expenditure policy are analyzed. In these chapters the theoretical notions discussed in Part Three are applied in evaluating the social

gains and costs of federal government spending and taxing policies. Part Four concludes with a discussion of the economics of
the public debt (Chapter 9).

Finally, in Part Five we take a brief look at some of the problems of political economy on which debate is currently focused.
These include the negative income tax proposals, the relationship of "tax expenditures" and tax credits to direct expenditures,
and the concept of the fiscal dividend and its allocation between
military and civilian budgets.

PART TWO

2

The Market System—Its Structure and Performance*

The private sector of the economy consists of the billions of daily exchanges of goods and services for money involving individual citizens or businesses. Participation in this sector is a familiar experience for each of us. Buying, selling, money, prices, consuming, producing—all of these are common in everyday life. This chapter will examine the basic principles which describe how the free market functions. As will be seen, the required properties that enable the system to perform in the public interest are rigorous ones. If they are not present in the real world, the operation of the market system breaks down and society must devise modes of collective decision making in order to attain its objectives.

I. THE MARKET SYSTEM—A SIMPLE MODEL

In order to cut through the welter of transactions and economic activities which compose the private market economy, we shall

---

* This chapter deals with some of the elementary principles of market analysis—the circular-flow model, supply and demand, equilibrium, the conditions for efficient market operation, and the answers provided by an ideal market system to the questions of What? How? and For Whom? As a review of material that is likely to be covered in another part of the introductory economics course, this chapter can be omitted with no loss of continuity.

build a simple economic model. In this model we shall discuss the behavior of the primary actors in the private sector—households and businesses—by abstracting from some of the complexities which they display in the real world. The essential features which motivate and determine their behavior will be retained, however. We shall introduce our discussion of the market system by examining households and business firms, then we shall discuss the markets in which they interact.

A. *Households*

For our purposes, a household is defined as any grouping of individuals which collectively decides both how they will earn their income and how they will spend it (or whether they will spend it). A number of important aspects of this definition must be spotlighted.

First, a household makes two basic kinds of decisions and both of them are related to its budget. It not only has to decide how much it is going to earn and how, but it also must decide how to allocate its earnings among the various spending possibilities. Not only must it decide, for example, whether or not the wife is going to work and whether or not the husband is going to "moonlight," but it must also worry about the allocation of its income between, say, a new car and the children's education or another package of doughnuts and a package of ground beef.

Second, a household deals in money—money is what is earned and what is spent. It is by means of money that the household values its possessions, stores its wealth, and evaluates its alternative purchases.

Third, households have something which they can sell. This must be so if they are to earn income and purchase goods and services. The basic things which households possess are called *factors of production*. These productive factors are the land, labor, and capital resources to which a household holds title. Households earn income when they sell the services of these factors for money.[1]

Finally, households must have some objective or goal that they

---

[1] When these factor services are sold, the income earned is called rent, wages, and interest, respectively.

attempt to achieve. Otherwise they would not worry about how they spend their money or how and how much they earn—one outcome would be as good as the next. We shall assume that whatever decisions the household makes, it makes them so as to gain as much satisfaction (or utility) as it can.

A household, then, is an independent grouping of people possessing the following essential characteristics.

1. A single decision maker.
2. The objective of maximum satisfaction.
3. A limited quantity of original factors of production—land, labor, and capital.
4. The freedom to sell the services of its factors to earn income.
5. The freedom to use its income to buy goods and services or acquire assets.

B. *Businesses*

For this discussion, a business will be known as an artificial creature which is owned by private individuals. It buys factors of production from households, it transforms these factors into goods and services, and it sells these outputs to households for money. This definition also contains several properties of businesses which must be noted.

First, a business, having decided what and how much it is going to produce, must also decide which factors of production or inputs it is going to buy and use in producing this output. It must, for example, decide how much machinery (capital) it is going to use relative to labor and if it is, say, a producer of combs, whether it is going to make them of hard rubber or plastic. As in the case of households, these decisions involve how to earn and how to spend money. They are, consequently, related to the budget of the business.

Second, businesses, like households, deal in money. Again, money serves as a means of holding wealth, as a means of measuring value and as the medium by which businesses buy and sell.

Third, again like households, businesses must have a goal. Not unexpectedly, we shall presume that the reason businesses exist is to make a profit—to secure an excess of income over costs.

Moreover, we shall claim that each business tries to earn as great a profit as it can through the process of buying factors and producing and selling goods.

A business firm, therefore, is a privately owned entity possessing the following essential characteristics.

1. A single decision maker.
2. The objective of maximum profits.
3. A technology by which it produces a particular output using inputs of land, labor, and capital.
4. The freedom to sell its output to earn revenue.
5. The freedom to use its revenue to buy productive factors.

C. Markets

To complete the model of the private economy, we shall set the business and household sectors into motion and discover that social institution through which they interact.

In Figure 2-1, a conceptual picture of the private economy is shown. This diagram depicts the economy to be a single, connected system in which households and businesses are linked by one pair of flows in the upper half of the picture and by another pair in the lower half. In the upper part of the picture, money and goods and services constitute the pair of flows—households are shown exchanging money with businesses for goods and services. In the lower loop, money and the services of productive factors constitute the two flows—businesses give money to

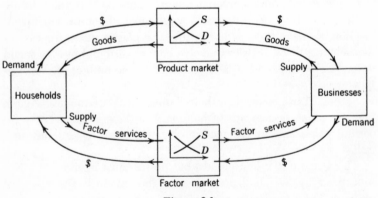

Figure 2-1

households in exchange for factor services. The flow of money from businesses to households is the *income* of the household. This income takes the form of wages for labor, interest for the services of capital (that is, plants, factories, tools, and machinery), and rent for the services of land. The upper loop shows that households, having received income, spend it to purchase goods and services. In the process, this flow of money becomes *revenue* to the business. Businesses, in turn, spend their revenue for the services of land, labor, and capital to enable them to produce their output. By purchasing the factors of production, businesses transform revenue into *costs of production* (except for what is left over, namely, *profits*).[2]

And so it goes, businesses and households interacting with each other in buying and selling final goods and factors of production in a circular-flow type system. Income spent by households becomes revenue to businesses who then allocate it to the purchase of factors of production. In the process, what was revenue to businesses becomes costs of production and, in turn, income to the households.

In the private economy, any place or any arrangement which enables the exchange of money for goods or services or for factors of production is a *market*. Thus, Figure 2-1 shows both the upper and lower loops passing through markets. It is not stretching the truth to call markets the vital link in the private economic system. Without markets, the basic ingredient of an exchange—the rate at which goods (or factors of production) exchange for money—would be missing. This exchange rate we call the *price*.[3] It is in a market that the price of items such as suits, cars, bananas, theater tickets, labor, land, and capital, is determined.

Markets are the "great reconcilers" of the private economy. In each market there are two groups of participants—buyers and sellers. The process of forming prices, of setting exchange ratios,

[2] In some more advanced presentations, profits are also treated as costs of production. The factor whose services they reward is called "entrepreneurship" or the "innovative capacity" of the owner of the firm.

[3] When we say, for example, that the price of an hour's worth of labor is $3 and the price of a pair of shoes is $18, we can automatically say, 1 pair of shoes is equivalent to 6 hours of labor. The price is the common denominator which establishes the rate of exchange between commodities.

is one of accommodating the wishes of both buyers and sellers; of getting them both to agree on a single price. The phenomenal thing about markets is that they undertake this reconciliation process automatically with no assistance from outside individuals or forces. This automatic process is described as the *Law of Supply and Demand.*

In the process of exchange, buyers, given their tastes, preferences, and incomes, make known in the market the intensity of their willingness to pay for a particular good or service. Similarly, sellers, given the structure of their costs, display in the market their willingness to make available certain quantities of their goods at various alternative prices. This willingness to buy and to sell is summarized in the standard demand (*DD*) and supply (*SS*) curves shown in Figure 2-2.

In the market, these opposite desires (or "willingnesses") confront each other. Sellers want high prices and are willing to increase the amount they are willing to sell only if the price goes

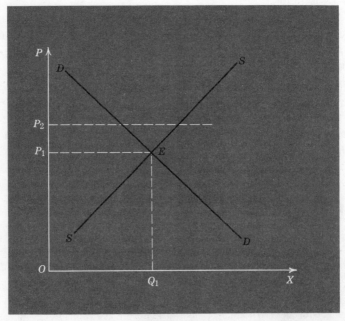

Figure 2-2

up. Conversely, buyers want low prices and will consent to increase their purchases only if the price goes down. In the market, the negatively inclined demand curve interacts with the positively sloped supply curve and an equilibrium price and quantity exchanged are determined. In Figure 2-2, this equilibrium price is P_1, the corresponding quantity is Q_1, and the equilibrium point at which the supply and demand curves intersect is denoted by E.[4]

Markets, then, are the crucial connecting link in the private sector of the economy. In markets, exchanges are made, prices are formed, and incomes, costs, and revenues are determined. Markets link buyer to seller, household to business, and provide the channel through which the circular flow of money, factor services, and commodities pass.

II. THE CONDITIONS FOR EFFICIENT MARKET OPERATION

A number of conditions must be met if the private sector of the economy—the market system—is to function efficiently. Indeed, these conditions are essential if the private sector is to perform in the public interest.[5] Because it is the absence of these conditions which often gives rise to demands for public sector (government) action, let us briefly describe the meaning of each.

A. *Perfect Competition in All Markets*

There must be perfect competition in the private economy if markets are to operate efficiently. Under this condition, every market has so many buyers and sellers that no single trader has any control over the price of the good or service which is being

---

[4] Were the price above P_1, say, at P_2, it could not be maintained. The amount sellers are willing to sell at that price is substantially greater than the amount buyers are willing to buy. In this situation, some sellers, unable to sell, would start to cut the price. This price cutting would force their competitors to follow and, hence, drive down the market price. Conversely, the market price would be driven up toward P_1 should it, for some reason, be placed below P_1. Hence, it is only at P_1 that the quantity supplied equals the quantity demanded and that there is no tendency for the price to change. P_1 is the equilibrium price and Q_1 is the equilibrium quantity.
[5] We shall state shortly what we mean by the "public interest."

exchanged. All buyers and sellers are price takers, not price makers. The price is made in the market through the impersonal forces of supply and demand.

If the market system is to function ideally, this kind of competition must prevail in all markets of the economy, both those for goods and services and those for factors of production. In those markets in which a single trader is important enough to affect price by exercising control over supply or demand, competition gives way to market power. If one or a few sellers have control over supply, the market is said to be *monopolistic*. If one or a few buyers have control over demand, the market is *monopsonistic*. Where market power prevails—either monopsony or monopoly power—the market does not perform its reconciliation function efficiently. The prices which result cause resources to be allocated differently than in the case of competition.[6]

B. *Increasing Costs in All Industries*

The existence of competition implies that each industry in the economy possesses increasing costs. Increasing costs mean that as any producer (business firm) in the economy grows larger, there is some output level at which his costs per unit begin to rise. If a steel firm were producing 100,000 tons of steel per year at $16 per ton and if its costs rose to $16.50 per ton when it increased output to 105,000 tons, it would be experiencing increasing costs. If increasing costs did not exist, the first producer of a commodity would find that his costs continually fell as he grew larger. Consequently, no firm beginning production after the first firm could be as efficient as the first firm. In such a situation, there would tend to be only one producer of a commodity. By definition, this means the absence of perfect competition. The situation in which costs are either decreasing or constant is referred to as a "natural monopoly." Monopoly is "natural" because the monopolist need do nothing on his own to subvert his competitors. He

[6] The economic analysis of monopoly demonstrates that when monopoly power is present: (1) price exceeds the marginal cost of production; (2) output is restricted from the ideal level; (3) insufficient resources (inputs) are attracted to the controlled market; and (4) monopolists are able to reap abnormal profits over a long period of time. It is these distortions in the competitive, circular flow economy to which we refer.

becomes a monopolist because the technology of his industry grants him continually falling costs.

C. *The Exclusion Property*

This property refers to a characteristic which goods, services, and factors of production must possess if a market system is to function ideally. For a good, service, or factor to be "exclusive," everyone but the buyer of the good must be excluded from the satisfactions it provides. A pair of sox, for example, is a good which is consistent with the exclusion principle. When you buy the sox, it is you alone who gets the satisfaction from wearing them—no one else. On the other hand, a shot for diptheria is a "commodity" which is *not* subject to the exclusion principle. While the person innoculated surely get benefits from having the shot, the benefit is not exclusively his. Having become immune to the disease, he can't communicate it to other people. They cannot be excluded from the benefit of the shot even though they do not pay for it and even though the person receiving the shot cannot charge them for it. Commodities which are not subject to the exclusion principle are said to possess *spillover* effects. Their benefits (and costs)[7] spill over onto third parties. When these effects are present, demand curves fail to capture the full "willingness-to-pay" and supply curves fail to capture the full costs. The demand curves, for example, would capture the willingness-to-pay of buyers of the good, but not the willingness-to-pay of those who are indirectly benefited through no action of their own. If this occurs, free market price signals will lead producers to produce too little or too much of the commodity. Prices developed in the market will lead to a misallocation of resources if the exclusion property does not hold.

D. *Absence of Public Goods*

Defined most simply, public goods are those which are not subject to the exclusion principle. However, they represent such an ex-

---

[7] As we shall see, costs as well as benefits can spill over onto third parties. Consider, for example, the "cost" which you incur when the person next to you in the park on a quiet Sunday afternoon plays his radio at full volume. It is likely that he will not offer to compensate you for the unpleasantness which he is causing.

treme case of "spillovers" that they deserve special treatment. Indeed, a public good can be said to be "all spillover"—as soon as one person gets the good, everybody gets it, and in equal quantity. Nobody can be excluded from it. A classic example of such a good is the ocean lighthouse. Once it is alive and blinking, all boats at sea can avail themselves of its services. No boat can be excluded. Another example is that "good" which we call "national defense." If one of a nation's citizens gets protected from foreign invasion, all do. As we shall see, if a good is a public good, it will not be produced privately and sold in the free market, even though it would be in society's interest to have it provided.

E. *Complete Knowledge*

For the private sector to operate ideally, all buyers and sellers must have full knowledge of all the alternatives available to them and the characteristics of these alternatives. With such knowledge, reconciliation of the willingness to pay of all those wanting a commodity with the willingness to sell of those supplying the commodity will be accomplished in markets. *Without* such knowledge, the "willingnesses" which are registered in markets would be only partial, since some people would be unaware of the full range of the alternatives. Having only a partial expression of demand and supply, the market cannot carry out the reconciliation function ideally. Again the resulting market prices would deviate from those which would occur with full knowledge.

F. *Complete Mobility*

If resources are mobile they will move in response to changes in prices. Consumer and producer decisions will be altered as observed market signals become modified. In fact, this is precisely what is implied by downward sloping demand curves and upward sloping supply curves. More will be demanded as prices fall and less will be supplied. In such an economy prices serve to channel resources and energies in response to changing demands and supplies.

In a completely mobile economy, each individual is prepared to alter his pattern of spending and earning income in response to changing prices. In searching for maximum satisfaction, completely mobile laborers would move freely among jobs as wage differentials developed. Mobile consumers would swiftly switch their trade from business to business as yesterday's high-price merchant becomes today's cheapest alternative. Businesses would respond to a decrease in the price of labor relative to the price of capital by substituting labor for capital. It is clear that this kind of flexibility is essential for the smooth operation of the market system. Without fluidity and mobility, prices would fail to serve their function as signalling devices. If decision makers were insensitive to price changes, the "invisible hand" of the market system would no longer guide society's resources into those uses in which they have the greatest social value.[8]

III. THE MARKET SYSTEM AND THE PUBLIC INTEREST

If all of these conditions are met, the private enterprise market system will function without a hitch. Indeed, it can be shown that if these conditions hold, there is no arrangement of the society's resources which will produce a real income greater than that generated by the market system. Because of this proposition, we can claim that the ideal market system operates in the public interest. The importance of this conclusion requires us to pursue it in greater detail.

All economic systems, it can be claimed, perform three basic functions, which are summarized by the questions: What? How? For whom? All economic systems determine *what* will be produced (the composition of the GNP), *how* it will be produced (the production methods and the allocation of labor, land, and capital among different outputs), and *who* will get the final output (the distribution of society's income). It can be argued, and in economics it has been for decades, that the ideal market system,

[8] It was Adam Smith, commonly known as the father of economics, who emphasized this point. "Every individual endeavors to employ his capital so that its produce may be of greatest value. He generally neither intends to promote the public interest, nor knows how much he is promoting it. He intends only his . . . own gain. And he is in this led by an *invisible hand* to promote an end which was no part of his intention. By pursuing his own interest he frequently promotes that of society more effectually than when he really intends to promote it." *The Wealth of Nations* (New York: Modern Library, Inc., originally published in 1776), p. 423.

with all of the above conditions satisfied, answers each of these questions in the best possible way.

A. *What?*

With a smoothly functioning market system, the complete pattern of consumer preferences is captured in the demands which are expressed in the market. Likewise, the costs to society of satisfying these preferences are embodied in the supply curves. Consequently, when the market reconciles demands and supplies, it enables everything which is produced to yield *benefits* to buyers (as reflected in their willingness to pay) which exceed the *costs* of getting it produced. Conversely, nothing gets produced for which the *costs* exceed the *benefits*. Thus, the ideal market system is responsive to the desires of the people as their desires are reflected in their willingness to pay. It insures that those worthwhile goods get produced which consumers want most.

B. *How?*

The market system will see to it that each of the final commodities which is produced will be produced most efficiently, that is, in the least costly way.[9] This occurs for at least two reasons. First, because of competition, the discovery of a better, less costly way of producing a commodity will be seized by all of the competitors in an industry. Each seeks to raise his profits by getting the jump on the competition. Indeed, because of competition, each firm is constantly pressed to discover more efficient ways to produce the goods in whose production it is specializing.

A second reason relates to how a business will choose to produce its product—how much capital it will use relative to labor. In its efforts to maximize profits, a business will never use another dollar's worth of labor if that unit fails to generate an extra dollar's worth of output. It will, however, use another dollar's worth of labor if it does generate more than a dollar's worth of output. Similarly with capital. Hence the profit motive will insure that no labor or capital will be employed in a use in which it fails to

[9] It should be stressed that there are usually a substantial number of ways of producing a product. Not only will the smoothly functioning market system seek out the most economical production process, it will, in addition, generate a search for new technologies and new processes of production.

produce at least as much as it is being paid. If each unit of output is, therefore, forced to "pay its way," our model of the ideal market system leads us to expect an efficient pattern of resource use and a minimum of economic waste.

C. *For Whom?*

While the distribution of society's output is tied up with ethical questions, it can be claimed that the market system performs well here too—that is, if you are prepared to accept a particular equity principle. If you believe that a man's income should be related to the contribution of his factor services to the society's output *and* if you find the initial distribution of capital, land, and labor among the people to be acceptable, it is possible to view the market system as an *efficient* means of answering the "for whom" question. As implied in the previous paragraph, the market system rewards each factor of production according to the value that the last unit used of that factor produces. Consequently, thinking of each unit as the last unit used, it can be claimed that each labor hour, each capital unit, and each parcel of land earns what it has contributed to the value of output. If "reward according to contribution" is an acceptable ethical basis for income distribution and if the initial distribution of factors (due in large part to inherited wealth and advantages) is not morally repugnant, the market system efficiently answers the "for whom" as well as the "what" and "how" questions.

IV. SUMMARY AND CONCLUSIONS

This chapter has reviewed the basic principles of market operation. The characteristics and objectives of both households and businesses were described as was the institution of the market in the private economy. Through the reconciliation of diverse interests accomplished by markets, prices are formed and serve as signaling devices. In responding to these signals, participants in the market system produce those goods and services which consumers most want and resources are allocated optimally among alternative uses. Each factor of production is rewarded in proportion to its contribution to total social output.

It was claimed that if the market system was functioning at its "efficient-best," it would serve the public interest better than any alternative arrangement. A number of characteristics have to exist, however, for the market system to function this way. There has to be the perfect competition in each market, implying an absence of decreasing costs; the exclusion property must be universal so that there are no benefit or cost spillovers onto third parties, and no public goods; there must be full knowledge of alternatives and perfect mobility. Only if all of these conditions hold will the market system be an efficient one—only under these conditions will it *efficiently* answer the what, how, for whom questions. Where these conditions fail to exist, demands for modification of the market outcome and abandonment of private decision making are generated. Collective action replaces individual action and government develops an economic function.

3

Market Failure and the Need for Collective Action

The list of requirements which must be met for a market system to operate efficiently is a long one—competition and increasing costs in all markets, the exclusion property, absence of public goods, and complete knowledge and mobility. It is difficult to read through it without sensing that the real world deviates from the ideal in a myriad of ways. Indeed, if the characteristics necessary for an ideal market system prevailed in the real world, the U.S. economy would not be the mixed public-private economy that it is. If there were no aberrations from the list, there would be no need for collective action to achieve goals. All economic activity would occur in the private sector.

In the real world, however, some economic goals can be attained only through collective action. Many markets are not perfectly competitive. Violations of the exclusion principle are a dime a dozen. In fact, some have argued that spillovers pervade our economic order. Lack of market knowledge and immobilities are commonplace in contemporary society. In short, the real world is rife with examples of how markets fail; examples of how the private sector, left to operate without social interference, would produce too much of some goods, too little of other goods, and none at all of still other socially worthwhile goods. In this chapter we shall discuss the extent of market failure in the real world and describe society's response to it.

I. MONOPOLY, DECREASING COSTS, AND ECONOMIC INEFFICIENCY

For competition in an industry to develop and flourish automatically, businesses must find it increasingly costly to grow beyond a size which is modest relative to the entire market. If an individual business fails to encounter increasing costs, there is no reason why it should ever stop growing.[1] A firm that experiences continuously decreasing unit costs will tend to absorb the entire market and become a monopoly.

Consequently, increasing costs are necessary to insure that there are several firms in an industry. As Chapter 2 described, a natural monopoly situation exists when increasing costs are absent. Such a monopoly, left free to operate in the market, will exhibit all of the traits characteristic of single suppliers attempting to maximize profits—it will restrict its output, raise its price, and impose what amounts to a private tax on the buyer of its output.

The decreasing cost-natural monopoly phenomenon is by no means rare in the U.S. economy. Indeed, on the basis of observed cost figures, several industries contain firms which display decreasing costs over a wide range of output. In a few industries, decreasing costs are so prominent that monopoly is the only technologically efficient arrangement. In a large number of other cases, increasing costs are sufficient to permit only a few firms to operate efficiently in an industry.

Industries in which only a few firms can operate efficiently are called *natural oligopolies*. A study conducted by Professor Joe Bain concluded that, of 20 prominent U.S. manufacturing industries (including petroleum refining, steel, and automobiles), about one-half showed such severe decreasing costs that only 10 or fewer "optimal" size firms could be absorbed. In these industries, oligopoly is decreed by the economies which come with large firm size.

Because of this decreasing cost phenomenon, society finds itself on the horns of a dilemma. If the force of competition is to be

---

[1] It should be noted that there are important reasons why firms experience lower unit costs as they grow larger. These are often referred to as "economies of mass production." In economics they are called "economies of scale."

effective, there must be a substantial number of firms in any market. However, when economies of scale are present, competition can be had only at the cost of substantial inefficiency. Society has resolved this dilemma in a number of different ways—antitrust legislation, public regulation, and simply "putting up with" noncompetitive markets.

In the case of *natural oligopolies* (for example, steel, petroleum, aluminum, tin cans, and autos) social constraints on the behavior of firms have been imposed. Laws forbidding monopolization and price-fixing have been passed and enforced, and the market behavior of these industries is persistently observed. In the federal government, these functions are performed by both the Anti-Trust Division of the Justice Department and the Federal Trade Commission. State and local governments also have price-fixing and antimonopoly legislation.[2]

In the U.S. economy, one finds examples of *natural monopoly* in the electric generating industry, much of the transportation industry (including railroads), the communications industry, and in the municipal water, gas, and electrical supply industries. As with oligopoly, the market fails to regulate these natural monopolies. Again, collective action is required to insure that these industries operate in the public interest.

In our economy, government commissions are used to regulate the market behavior of the communications, transportation, and electric utility industries—hence, the Federal Communications Commission, the Interstate Commerce Commission, the Federal Power Commission, and a large number of state regulatory commissions. For some of these industries, we have decided that public ownership rather than regulation is the best arrangement. Many cities, for example, own and operate their own water, electrical, and sewer systems.

II. SPILLOVERS AND ECONOMIC INEFFICIENCY

In a modern and increasingly complex society, the nature of goods, services, and production and consumption processes results

[2] For a further discussion of monopoly and oligopoly industry structure, see *Case Studies in American Industry*, by Leonard Weiss, in this series.

in frequent negation of the exclusion principle.[3] It does not require unusual perception to recognize the pervasiveness of external effects and spillovers. Indeed, whenever someone inflicts a "harm" on another person without compensating him, or aids him without being compensated, there exists a spillover cost or benefit and a violation of the exclusion property.

When the meat-packing firm dumps its unused animal parts into a river, downstream swimmers and fishermen are the objects of spillover costs; when your next-door neighbor plays his phonograph loudly and it annoys you, you are the object of a spillover cost; when the coal-burning industry in a community fills the sky with coal dust smog, residents of the community are the objects of a spillover cost; when the next semitruck pulls onto the freeway with the effect of delaying your arrival and that of all other freeway motorists, you and your fellow drivers are the objects of a spillover cost. It is characteristic that in each of these cases, the person harmed bears identifiable "costs" for which he is *not* compensated. Moreover, in each case, this person would be willing to pay something to avoid bearing the spillover cost.

Spillover benefits, like spillover costs, abound in the real world. These external benefits occur when one party's action provides a "gain" to someone else for which payment is not required. When a business hires and trains an otherwise unskilled worker, it is likely that the firm will not recover the full value of the worker's training—especially if the worker changes jobs. To the extent that the investment is not recovered, other people—the next employer and others—gain spillover benefits because of the training provided by the first employer. Similarly, if one property owner landscapes his property, plants trees and flowers, and resods his lawn, his neighbors reap some of the benefit in the form of a pleasant view for which they are not required to pay. They are the recipients of a spillover benefit. Or consider the case of a private electric utility which decides that the construction of a new reservoir for the production of hydropower would be a worthwhile investment. In building the reservoir, a fine swimming, boating, and fishing area is made available to recreationists.

[3] On page 25, we defined the exclusion principle as follows: "For a good . . . to be 'exclusive,' everyone but the buyer of the good must be excluded from the satisfactions it provides."

This latter group is the recipient of a spillover benefit. On the other hand, if the utility, by damming the river, destroys a beautiful and scenic view, those people who might otherwise have enjoyed the view are the objects of a spillover cost.

Because spillover costs and benefits pervade the economy, some people get hurt and others get helped through no action of their own. One of the serious issues related to spillovers, then, is an equity concern. Who is it that benefits from a spillover and who bears the cost? However, in addition to this equity impact, spillovers distort the allocation of society's resources. Either too much or too little will be produced of a good whose use generates spillover costs or benefits. This last proposition concerning economic efficiency is not so easy to understand. Let us discuss the economic effects of spillovers.

A. *The Economics of Spillovers*

As we pointed out in Chapter 2, the free market reaches an equilibrium where the supply and demand curves intersect. At this equilibrium, the price of the commodity or service is determined as is the quantity of it which will be produced and exchanged. This equilibrium equates the willingness of buyers to pay for the good—reflected in the demand curve—with the cost of producing the good—reflected in the supply curve. Thus, at, and only at, the equilibrium price P_1 in Figure 3-1, the amount which buyers are willing to pay for the last or marginal unit of X just equals the cost of producing that last unit—marginal benefit equals marginal cost. If all of the benefits of the good were included in the demand curve and if all of its costs were included in the supply curve, this equilibrium would be ideal. To produce one more unit beyond Q_1 would entail more cost than the value of the benefits it would create; to stop producing before Q_1 would leave some gains unexploited. For example, if production were stopped at Q_0, society would not secure the excess of gains over costs (ab) from producing the next unit.

Where there are spillovers, however, not all of the gains and costs are included in the market demand and supply curves. For spillover benefits, there is a willingness to pay in addition to that which is captured in the demand curve. In Figure 3-2, for example, we have a model in which units of education are plotted on the *x* axis and dollars per unit are plotted on the *y* axis. The willingness to pay for education by its potential buyers is included in the demand curve *DD*. At very high prices, they are willing to buy less education than at lower prices. Their willingness to pay reflects their evaluation of the worth of education *to them*—higher incomes over their lifetime, the satisfaction gained from broad knowledge and educational experience, and so on. The costs of providing education are shown in the supply

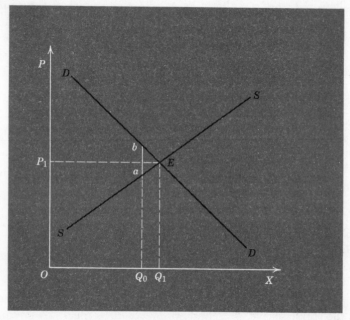

Figure 3-1

curve *SS*—at a low price, fewer units of education would be forthcoming than at higher prices. In a free market, Q_1 units of education would be produced and exchanged.

Education, however, involves spillover benefits. Other people benefit in addition to the purchasers of education. The general population benefits if John Doe gets educated because an educated John Doe is less likely to be a juvenile delinquent; John Doe's family benefits because they are less likely to have to support him if he becomes sick or unemployed; the nation as a whole benefits because an educated citizenry provides it with economic growth opportunities and social stability which it would not otherwise have. If these spillover benefits are added to the willingness to pay which is expressed in the market (the demand curve *DD*), the total willingness to pay is shown as *TT* in Figure 3-2. In the diagram, there exists a spillover benefit of $b per unit of education.[4]

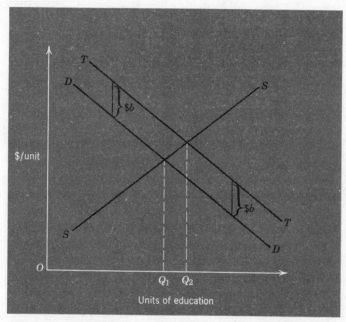

Figure 3-2

As can now be seen, the existence of the spillover benefit results in an insufficient output if the market is free to function un-

[4] The spillover benefit of $b per unit is ascertained in the same way that the demand curve was derived. In deriving the demand curve, all of the purchasers of the good were asked how much they would be willing to pay for each of a number of quantities of the good. In deriving spillover benefits, all of the people who *indirectly* find themselves better off because a good is produced are asked how much they would be willing to pay rather than forego the spillover benefit. In Figure 3-2 this amount is $b per unit.

obstructed. While the free market equilibrium would yield an output of Q_1, it is in the interest of society to have Q_2 units of education produced. At Q_1, the next unit of output yields benefits in excess of costs and, hence, it is in the social interest to get that additional unit produced. Consequently, *where spillover benefits exist, the free market produces an output which is smaller than the socially optimum output.* Only if output is carried to Q_2 are marginal costs equated with *total* marginal benefits.

The reverse of this situation occurs where spillover costs are present. This is shown in Figure 3-3. When there are spillover costs, the supply curve fails to capture all of the social costs of producing the output. Consider, for example, the case of the meat processor who pollutes a river. While the supply curve (SS) captures all of the private costs of processing meat, the water pollution costs which spill over onto the rest of society are not captured. These costs may take the form of reduced catches for

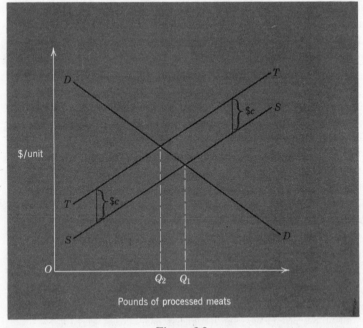

Figure 3-3

fishermen or decreased swimming opportunities for recreationists. If these spillover costs are added to the private costs, the total social cost of processing meat is given by TT in Figure 3-3. This includes a spillover cost of $\$c$ per unit of meat produced. Again in this case the free unobstructed market fails to get the optimum quantity of output produced. From society's point of view, Q_2 is the optimum output level but the free market generates a greater output of Q_1 units. *In the case of spillover costs, the free market output is greater than the optimum output which takes into account total social costs and gains.* All units of output beyond Q_2 involve marginal social costs in excess of marginal social benefits.

This existence of spillovers, then, implies an "incorrect" or nonoptimal level of output if the free market is permitted to operate unobstructed. In the case of spillover benefits, buyers, acting on the basis of their own private gains, convey to the market a demand (DD) which is less than that which would have been conveyed if total social gains (TT) had been reflected (Figure 3-2). In the case of spillover costs, sellers, acting on the basis of their own private costs, supply an output (SS) which is greater than the willingness to supply would have been if total social costs had been reflected in the seller's costs (Figure 3-3). In both cases, the wrong output (from society's point of view) results because individual decision makers behave on the basis of *private* costs and gains—which deviate from *total social* costs and gains. In the case of spillover benefits, too few of society's resources are allocated to the free market production of the good in question (and, hence, too many resources are allocated to the other goods produced in the economy.) The opposite occurs in the case of free market production of goods with spillover costs. There, too many of society's resources are allocated to the good in question. In these cases, there is misallocation of resources, economic inefficiency, and a free market performance which fails to conform to the social optimum.

B. *Spillovers and Collective Action*

When significant spillovers are found in the real world, collective action, usually through a government, becomes necessary if efficient performance is to be secured.[5] The possible forms of public action are many. However, all of these actions are designed to eliminate the inefficiencies caused by spillovers by getting the "optimal" quantity of output produced. The responsibility of public action is to adjust the nonoptimal output levels generated by the imperfectly operating free market.

One of the more drastic forms of public sector action occurs when a government takes over an industry in which spillovers are prevalent. In this way the public sector can insure that the "ideal" output gets produced. This has been the solution which the United States has chosen in the case of primary and secondary education. In part because of spillovers, our society has chosen a system of public education.[6] For much the same reason, governments operate police forces, fire departments, and public health facilities.

Another form of public action is to impose a special charge (tax) on industries that are imposing spillover costs and to make a special payment (subsidy) to industries that generate spillover benefits. The effect of the special charge in the spillover cost case is to force the firms who are imposing the spillover to include the otherwise neglected cost in their own private calculation. By "internalizing" the spillover cost through a special charge, the firms will be led to make decisions on the basis of total social

[5] It needs to be emphasized that not all observed spillovers require government corrective action. A helpful distinction is that between "real" spillovers and what are called money or "pecuniary" spillovers. In the case of real spillovers, some real output or consumption or satisfaction is produced or destroyed without people being compensated. Pecuniary spillovers involve simply a loss of income to one person, which income is transferred to another person. For example, when competition causes a railroad to cut rates, passengers are benefited and the railway owners are hurt. The new competition grants a spillover benefit to passengers—however, it imposes an offsetting spillover cost on the railway owners. This redistribution of income involves *pecuniary* spillovers and not real ones. Indeed, the ongoing operation of the market system produces pecuniary spillovers as an essential part of its giving market signals through changing prices. Government corrective action can safely ignore these transfer (or money or pecuniary) spillovers. It is the real spillovers on which it must concentrate.

[6] It should be emphasized that there are economic and noneconomic reasons in addition to spillovers which account for the "nationalization" of elementary and secondary education.

costs rather than just those private costs which they incur. If the special charge (at the margin) is equal to the amount of the spillover, private decision makers will tend naturally to make the socially correct output decision.

Similarly, firms generating spillover benefits can be induced to produce the correct output if they are granted a special, compensating payment. The investment tax credit legislation passed by the federal government has been defended on these grounds. By encouraging businesses to invest more in a period of high unemployment through a special "payment" for investing, firms are compensated for doing something which has significant social or spillover benefits.

A third social instrument to deal with spillovers is the administrative regulation. By administrative or legislative ruling, the action which causes the spillover can be prohibited. Smoke ordinances are common examples. Their purpose is to eliminate those actions of private persons and enterprises which impose spillover costs on third parties and to internalize those costs. Much of the recent water pollution control legislation by the federal government entails this form of public sector action, as does the federal legislation dealing with exhaust control devices currently installed on new cars.[7]

A fourth way of attempting to ameliorate some of the undesirable effects of spillover costs is through the power of persuasion. Thus, families are urged by the government to get shots for communicable diseases, such as polio and diptheria. Similarly, firms emitting industrial wastes into the atmosphere are cajoled by state, local, and federal governments to "take seriously their civic responsibilities."

Finally, the public sector has often reacted to spillover costs by spending money to mitigate or reduce the effect of the spillover on other people. For those spillover costs created by people who throw refuse out of their automobiles on scenic roads, the government hires road crews to clean up the results of the spillover-causing behavior. To erase the aesthetic scars caused by massive

[7] Another example of a ruling to eliminate spillover-causing activity occurred in July, 1969 when the California State Senate passed a bill stating that, by 1975, no new cars sold in that state would be permitted to have an internal combustion engine.

highway construction projects and the ugliness of private junk-yards built along the roadside, the public sector undertakes large-scale beautification programs. One hears increasing talk about what the government can do to correct the undesirable effects of the private and public sectors' pollution of the nation's rivers and streams. The alternative public actions that have been discussed include the building of dams to increase the flow of the river in periods of low flow, the construction (or subsidization) of waste disposal plants, and the insertion into rivers of large pieces of equipment designed to pump oxygen into badly polluted streams so as to reduce some of the undesirable effects of the pollution load. All of these represent government spending to erase the harmful effect caused by private (and sometimes public) behavior.

It should be emphasized that while some of these types of public action eliminate the third-party effects, they fail to correct the excess or insufficient output of the spillover-causing behavior. Private decision makers still make their decisions on only a portion of the total social costs or benefits involved. This is particularly true of the "administrative regulation" and "governmental corrective action" solutions.

III. PUBLIC GOODS AND MARKET FAILURE

As mentioned in Chapter 2, public goods are the extreme case of goods with spillover effects. Instead of violating the exclusion property in a limited way, public goods violate it with a vengeance. No one can be excluded from the benefits once the public good is produced. While public goods are not nearly so prominent in the real world as goods with less extreme spillover effects, neither are they rare occurrences. The posting of signs on a highway, for example, is a public good. The benefits cannot be denied to anyone who travels the road. Similarly, when a society provides national defense, the benefits accrue to all of its citizens. Because it is so costly to ration the system of city streets once it has been put into place, they, too, are public goods.

Because one can not economically be excluded from the benefits of a public good once it has been provided, private firms have no incentive to produce and market these commodities.

Any potential buyer would refuse to pay anything like what the commodity is worth to him. Indeed, he would be likely to express an unwillingness to pay anything at all for it. He would reason: "If I simply sit tight and refuse to pay, I may get the benefit of the good anyway, if someone down the line provides it for himself—after all, it is a public good." However, if each buyer reasons this way (and presumably he will), the good will not be provided. Public goods will only be provided if collective action, usually through a government, is taken. Only through collective action can the availability of worthwhile public goods be assured.

The existence of public goods (that is, goods with extreme spillover effects) in the real world is, therefore, another reason why the market system fails. Their existence provides an additional economic rationale for the range of economic activities undertaken by government.

IV. IMMOBILITIES, IMPERFECT KNOWLEDGE, AND MARKET FAILURE

While the "ideal" market system displays mobility of both buyers and sellers, and knowledge of all alternatives, the absence of these qualities in the real world hardly needs documentation. Workers are seldom (if ever) aware of the full range of available employment alternatives. Indeed, in most cases, they search out only a handful of options and then only when they contemplate making a change of jobs. This is even more true when job alternatives involve movement from one city to another, or movement from the farm to the city. In such moves, the problem of imperfect knowledge is compounded by significant noneconomic ties causing a lack of mobility.[8] Much the same holds true for businesses when they consider locations or the purchase of inputs, and for households when they spend their income to purchase goods and services.[9]

The public sector, through specific government services, has

---

[8] Adam Smith once observed that ". . . man is of all forms of luggage the most difficult to be transported."

[9] It should be noted, however, that when the procurement of information entails costs, the economic optimum consists of less than full knowledge of all alternatives.

tried to counter this lack of knowledge and existence of immobilities. In this way, government has strengthened the private sector by developing those things necessary to make it run efficiently. For example, the federal government publishes an enormous volume of statistics relating to economic or market conditions. All of these have the purpose of providing to households and businesses more and better information, thus enabling them to make better business and household decisions. For example, the federal government provides regular agricultural market forecasts, including prediction of future supplies, demands, and prices. These enable farmers to make more enlightened decisions on what to produce and when and where to market it.

Both the state and federal governments perform much the same function with respect to the problem of labor immobility. All states maintain employment centers that give labor market information to unemployed workers or to workers looking for a change in jobs. This information makes movement among alternatives more likely than it otherwise would be. Similarly, the U.S. Department of Labor provides substantial assistance to migrant workers in aiding them to locate those regions with the highest potential employment opportunities.

In a very real sense, recent Civil Rights legislation has tended to reduce the immobility present in the U.S. economy. It has done so by opening up to black people a number of alternatives in housing markets, employment markets, and markets for goods and services which were previously foreclosed by artificial constraints. This legislation has probably had the most far-reaching impact on the existence of immobility of any public sector action in the last few decades. As such, it has made a significant contribution in the effort to increase the performance of the U.S. market system.

V. ECONOMIC JUSTICE AND COLLECTIVE ACTION

Thus far in our discussion, the economic rationale for government activity has been based on shortcomings in the operation of the market system. In each instance we argued that government action was necessary to correct or mitigate the consequences of market failure. However, in addition to these "efficiency" bases for collective action, there is another economic justification for government activities which is not related to a breakdown in the technical *operation* of the market system. This motivation stems from the society's rejection of the way in which the market system distributes income. As such, it is based on an *ethical* judgment and not on market failure.

As has been noted, the free market system automatically answers the "for whom," or income distribution, question. It does so by relating a man's income to the value which he (or the factors which he owns) contribute to the social product. Stated most simply, the market system provides very large incomes to those whose labor commands a high price and those who possess particularly valuable land and capital. The market system deals harshly with those of modest skill who are without any accumulated or inherited possessions.

A society has every right to reject that distribution of income which is automatically formed by the market system. One basis for adjusting the income distribution is a judgment on the desirability of the actual pattern which results from the operation of the system. A situation in which there are a few very rich people and a mass of impoverished citizens may well violate the ethical sensibilities of a majority of the people—including a majority of the rich. A second reason to alter the distribution of income produced by a market system is a rejection of the "reward according to contribution" principle on which the market system operates. One may well judge that peoples' standard of living should not be determined solely by the productivity of their labor and possessions, many of which are likely to be inherited. It is important to note that a market society can modify the distribution of income without disturbing the operation of the market system.

In the United States, a substantial number of government activities have income redistribution as their primary function. The social security system supports the elderly at the expense of people under 65. The unemployment insurance program supports the worker who cannot find a job at the expense of the employed. The Medicare Program supports the aged sick at the expense of the healthy, younger members of society. The income tax structure takes a greater proportion of the earnings of the high income class than it does of the poor. Indeed, current proposals for a negative income tax argue that only those above a certain income level should be taxed—those below that level would receive a payment. All of these are examples of actual or proposed governmental activities undertaken because of society's ethical rejection of the distribution of income dictated by the price system. They are based on a desire to alter the distribution of income toward one which is judged to be more socially desirable—as that judgment is reflected through the political process.

VI. SUMMARY AND CONCLUSIONS

In this chapter we presented a catalogue of the circumstances under which the market system breaks down. We argued that this market failure is a primary rationale for a large proportion of government activity. We elaborated why people turn to collective action to attain those objectives which cannot be satisfied efficiently through individual decisions in a price system.

In addition to this *efficiency* rationale for government programs, we cited the *equity* reason for collective action. The desire for a redistribution of society's income can only be satisfied by a government with (at least) the power to tax certain people and subsidize others. To be sure, this "economic justice" or equity motivation for governmental action is fully as potent in rationalizing government action as the pure efficiency arguments— some would argue that as our society grows more affluent and can afford more inefficiency and waste, the equity rationale will (and should) become even more prominent.

PART THREE

4

The Principle of Maximum Social Gain— A Framework for Analysis

In Parts One and Two, we concentrated on the private economy. We analyzed the operation of the market system, the conditions under which it would perform in the public interest, and the circumstances which would generate inefficiencies, market failure, and inequities. Because the private economy sometimes fails to operate in the public interest, sometimes fails to achieve an efficient allocation of society's resources, and sometimes generates an income distribution which violates ethical sensibilities, collective action through a public sector is required. This chapter examines the public sector.

Our objective here is to present a set of simple theoretical principles for evaluating the economic impact of public sector decisions and judging their effectiveness. The standard for judging the economic worth of public decisions is the same as that applied to private sector performance—do the people of the society gain more than they lose because of the decision? Is the increase in economic value caused by the decision greater than the economic cost that it imposes? In both this chapter and the next, we shall discuss the meaning of this standard in the context of government decisions.

I. PUBLIC SECTOR RECEIPTS AND EXPENDITURES

In economics, discussion of the effects of government decisions is contained in the literature of a field of study called public finance. This is so because the losses and gains caused by most government decisions are closely related to how the government gains and spends income and on how much income it decides to raise and spend.

The receipts of the public sector are overwhelmingly in the form of taxes of one sort or another.[1] Through taxes, the public sector forcibly[2] takes money from citizens which they could otherwise have used for their own private benefit. Citizens cede some buying power, some control over resources, some means of increasing their utility through market transactions, when they pay taxes. In analyzing the effects of public sector decisions, then, we must be concerned with the repercussions resulting from the imposition of taxes on the members of the private economy.

While taxes force the private economy to sacrifice some of its control over resources, that is only half the picture. Governments do not exact buying power from private citizens and then turn around and dump it down a rat hole. Rather, governments use their revenue to buy things which have value to the members of society—usually things which private citizens could not secure except through collective action.[3] That is to say, government spending, through its purchase and provision of things of value

[1] Some of the taxes raised by the public sector are not collected in the form of money. Even in our contemporary society, the public sector extracts some payments-in-kind, that is, payments in the form of real goods and services. For example, to the extent that market salaries exceed military pay, compulsory military service represents a "tax" paid by servicemen. United States practice with regard to jury service is another "tax-in-kind." People serving on juries could be earning far more in other activities than by jury duty. In effect, they donate a part of the market value of their services to the government.

[2] While use of the word "forcibly" is technically correct in that the government has a constitutional right to levy taxes, it should be recognized that the members of society are forcing themselves when they, through their representatives, pass tax legislation.

[3] Some of the objects of public expenditure may, however, appear to be of this rat-hole variety. For example, the $n billion paid for bombs dropped in Vietnam may be a complete waste—a waste of $n billion worth of resources which could have been used by private citizens for their own uses. There are some, however, who would defend this expenditure as having the value of defending the nation, stopping communism, or sustaining the existence of an independent nation under attack.

to the people of a society, creates an offset to the utility losses which are entailed by taxes.

In discussing the economic worth of public decisions, then, both the tax and the expenditure sides of the ledger must be looked at and compared. Moreover, one must look more deeply than simply at the dollar volume of a tax and the dollar value of an additional public expenditure. By themselves, these dollar volumes give little indication of the economic worth of a decision to, say, tax one more dollar and spend it on the space program.[4] Rather, one must inquire into real effects of taxes on the economy and compare these with the real effects of public expenditures. A government expenditure decision is in the public interest only if the burden caused by the taxes necessary to pay for it is less than the social value of the output which the expenditure provides.[5] Thus, the decision by the local school board to spend an additional $100,000 on public education may or may not be in the public interest depending on the real burden of raising $100,000 in taxes and the effects of a $100,000 increase in the school budget. Sir Hugh Dalton described this comparison well when he stated:

It is not possible to pass a complete judgment upon any . . . [government operation] without balancing against one another both sides of the operation, the effects of raising and the effects of the spending of public revenue.

[4] Indeed, if a government balances its budget (its income equalling its spending), the dollars coming in will equal the dollars going out. Using these flows as a guide would lead to a conclusion of *no* net gain from government spending and taxing. The number of dollars spent just equals the number of dollars taxed.

[5] The necessity for this kind of comparison in reaching a judgment on the worth of a public decision differs substantially from the simplistic position which has as its slogan, "The best government is the least government." This position, it should be noted, is not a new one. About 170 years ago a famous economist, J. B. Say, stated: "The very best of all plans of finance is to spend little and the best of all taxes is that which is least in amount." While this proposition defines "economy in government" to mean shrinking the size of government to some absolute physical minimum, the kind of comparison described in the text does not. Our comparison implies an effort to seek the right size government undertaking the right functions in the right amounts. This may entail expanding some public programs and cutting back others, expanding all programs, or cutting all back—depending on the gains-losses comparison.

II. A SIMPLE PUBLIC SECTOR MODEL

The operation of the public sector can be viewed as a series of transfers of buying power from private individuals to public authorities, and then a series of transfers from public authorities back to individuals. This process is depicted in Figure 4-1. There it is shown that control over some buying power is shifted to the government when it levies taxes on the private sector. In turn, the government either allocates this revenue to income transfer programs supporting some groups in the private sector or it uses the buying power itself to directly purchase goods and services. In the second case, the goods and services purchased are transformed into public sector outputs which yield benefits to people in the private sector.

A contemporary example of the first way in which government uses its revenue is the social security program. People under 65 who are working pay a certain amount of their income into a fund according to a fixed formula. Older people who are no longer working are able to draw funds out. A direct transfer occurs. The federal government is the institution through which purchasing power passes from those paying into to those drawing out of the social security fund. These direct government payments of money to people who fulfill certain requirements are called *transfer payments*.

The second means of transferring government-raised revenue is quite different from the transfer payment mechanism. While in the transfer payment case, some people receive a direct money payment, this is not so in the case of *exhaustive expenditures*. Here the public sector itself uses the revenue to purchase goods and services in the market. The government then transforms these goods and services into public outputs and supplies them directly to the private sector. Police and fire protection, high-

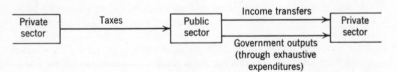

Figure 4-1

ways, public health facilities, and schools are examples of this second kind of public expenditure. The taxes given up by the private sector are used to produce public outputs or benefits which are of value to members of the private sector.[6]

III. THE PRINCIPLE OF MAXIMUM SOCIAL GAIN

For each of these two basic ways of disposing of government revenue—transfer and exhaustive expenditures—there is one question which is of paramount economic importance. Is the society better off because of the tax-expenditure combination or is it not? Are the gains from the tax-spending transaction greater than the losses or are they not? The comparison which is implied by this question is a basic one and can be summarized in a general principle—*The Principle of Maximum Social Gain;*

> *The public sector, in undertaking any activity, should choose that alternative for which the gains to society exceed the costs by the greatest amount and should refrain from any activity if its costs are not exceeded by gains.*

There are two important aspects of this principle to be emphasized. First, the principle states a minimum test which any public sector activity must meet if it is to be in the public interest. This test requires that any proposed public undertaking demonstrate prospective benefits which exceed anticipated costs before it is approved. Even if there is market failure in the private sector, a proposed "output" should not be produced by the government unless it can pass this minimum test. If the government should undertake an expenditure failing this test, it would be extracting *higher* valued resources from the private sector and devoting them to *lower* valued uses—the costs of the undertaking would exceed the gains. This would, on balance, decrease the economic welfare of the society.

[6] There is yet another important way in which the federal government disposes of its revenue. In a number of areas there exist grant-in-aid programs. Through these programs, federal revenues are transferred to either state or local governments. The programs for which the grants were established—public health, highways, education—are then undertaken by the lower level of government. Typically, grant-in-aid programs are an indirect way of carrying out direct exhaustive expenditures.

Second, for those public undertakings which pass the minimum justification test, the Principle of Maximum Social Gain imposes additional demands. To attain maximum social gain, the public decision maker must make a complete search of alternative ways of accomplishing the objective and must choose that alternative which *maximizes the excess of social gains over social costs.* Thus, if the decisionmaker faces two alternatives—*A*, with $25,000 gain and $10,000 cost, and *B*, with $35,000 gain and $15,000 cost —he should pick alternative *A* which yields the greater excess of gains over losses.

This principle incorporates the fundamental economic criterion for appraising any decision—public or private. It requires an estimation of the costs and gains that are generated by each alternative and a choice of the one which generates the largest net gain.

We have already used this principle in evaluating the operation of the market system. When spillovers are present, for example, we saw that the market fails to register all of the costs or gains. Because all of the costs or gains are not represented, the market generates erroneous signals and conveys them to buyers and sellers. They, in turn, behave so as to elicit a level of output in which net gains are not maximized. The result is a misallocation of resources. This maximum net gain test must also be applied to public sector decisions.

A. Social Costs and Social Gains

In analyzing government decision making, the meaning of social costs and gains must be clearly understood. At this point, their conceptual meaning will be emphasized; later we shall worry about how to measure them.

The benefits and costs of any public decision are of two basic types: *efficiency* benefits and costs and *income redistribution* (*equity*) benefits and costs.

First, let us consider the efficiency impacts. The notion of economic efficiency relates to the allocation of the society's resources. If the society's land, labor, and capital are allocated in the best possible way, the economic welfare of a society (its real GNP) will be as great as it can possibly be. A government activity, therefore, can increase the efficiency of an economy only if it can jiggle resources around so that they produce a greater real GNP. It does this if it can find a way to take resources out of the private sector which are valued at $X and use them to produce something worth $(X + 1)$ or $(X + 2)$ or more. The efficiency comparison, then, is between the value to the private sector of what it is forced to give up to support a government undertaking (represented by the tax-cost[7]) and the value of the output which the government provides with the resources taken from private citizens (represented by the willingness of the citizens to pay for the government-produced output, if they had to). Thus, the *efficiency* of the government's construction of a public park is demonstrated if the tax-cost of the park is $300,000 and if citizens would be willing to pay *more than* $300,000 to gain the enjoyment provided by the park.

The second kind of impact from public sector activity is the income redistribution impact. As pointed out in Chapter 3, achieving the income distribution most desired by society is also a responsibility of the public sector. However, an evaluation of this impact necessitates an ethical judgment—one has to say that a dollar going to some people is worth more to society than a dollar going to other people.

Most people are prepared to accept the proposition that a dollar which goes to a rich man produces less social welfare than a dollar which goes to a poor man. Although this proposition cannot be proven logically, we are going to accept it as true in our discussion. The implication of this proposition must be clearly understood: it means that a dollar taken from a rich man and given to a poor man "costs" society less than it "benefits" society. Such a transfer, therefore, is in the public interest.

These efficiency and income redistribution (or equity) impacts of government decisions are better understood by working through a couple of simple models. These artificial constructs are designed both to illustrate and to add precision to the Principle of Maximum Social Gain. The first case will deal with economic

---

[7] It must be emphasized that the dollar volume of taxes are not the real cost of a federal undertaking. Rather, it is the value of the things that private citizens would have spent their tax money on—cars, clothes, houses. However, in a smoothly functioning economy, the volume of taxes raised is likely to be a good estimate of the value of these opportunities foregone.

efficiency by asking the basic question: "What is the optimal size of the public sector?" In the second case, a model for thinking about the equity impacts of a public sector transfer program will be presented.

B. Model I—The Optimal Size of Government

The question of the size of the public sector is a problem of resource allocation. How many of society's resources should be allocated to the production of public sector goods relative to private sector goods? The Principle of Maximum Social Gain can assist in thinking meaningfully about this question. Let us make some assumptions and then apply the principle.

First, assume that all of the markets existing in the private sector are operating ideally—that there are no spillovers, decreasing costs, immobilities, and so on. Second, assume that there are some public goods that the private sector cannot produce and for which there are no private markets. It is these public goods which will comprise the government's activities. Finally, assume that the government has evaluated all of the alternative ways of producing all possible quantities of these public goods and that it knows the value of social benefits which will be generated from each dollar allocated to each alternative.

In Figure 4-2, for example, the total social value of constructing and operating public parks is related to the dollars of costs devoted to producing this public good. This relationship is depicted by curve *TSV*. This total social value (*TSV*) curve shows that for the first million dollars the government spends on parks, there is a very large social value, but as additional dollars are spent, the amount of value generated by each additional million dollars becomes smaller. This conclusion follows from the shape of the *TSV* curve which flattens out as more and more dollars are devoted to public parks.[8]

Because the government in this model has detailed social value information on all of the alternative public expenditure categories available to it, it is able to derive the total social value curve for expenditures on the full range of public sector alternatives. This

[8] In Figure 4-2, the first million dollars spent generates an increment to social value of *oa* while the 301st million dollars spent generates an increment to social value of only *bc*.

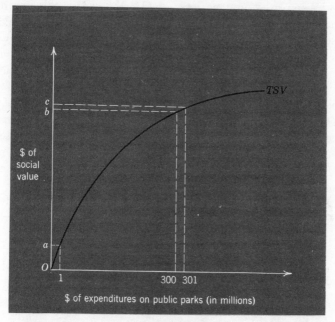

Figure 4-2

total social value curve (*TSV*) for the entire public sector is shown in Figure 4-3*a*.[9] On the same figure, the total social cost curve (*TSC*) is drawn.[10] The size of the government measured in terms of either the taxes that it raises or its spending is shown along the horizontal axis.

The basic question can now be put. How large should the government be? How much should it spend and tax? It is in answering this question that the Principle of Maximum Social Gain is relevant. As will be recalled, this principle instructs the decision maker to proceed until the excess of gains over costs from an activity are maximized. From inspection of Figure 4-3*a*, it is seen that to be true to the principle, the government budget should

---

[9] Here we are presuming that each additional dollar taken from the private sector and devoted to the public sector is spent on that public output which produces the greatest increase in social value.

[10] This curve is a straight 45° line because dollars of cost are plotted on both the horizontal and vertical axes. Implicit in this curve is the proposition that $1 of taxes entails $1 of social cost.

be *OA*—no more and no less. At *OA*, the excess of gains over costs (net gain) is *bc*, which is the greatest *vertical* distance that exists between these two curves. If government spending were less than *OA*, there would be some potential net gains which were not being realized. If the budget were larger than *OA*, some of the last dollars spent would entail social costs in excess of the benefits which they were producing.

This same result is shown in Figure 4-3*b*, which is derived from Figure 4-3*a*. In the lower panel the "marginal" curves—

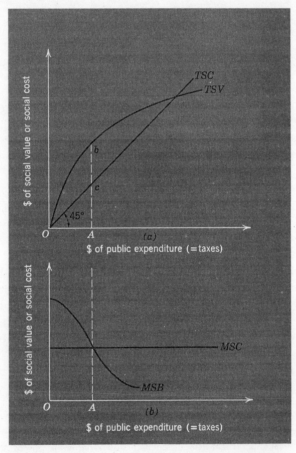

Figure 4-3

marginal social value (*MSV*) and marginal social cost (*MSC*)—associated with the "total" curves of the upper panel are drawn. There the proposition so familiar in economics is seen applied to the public sector: *net gain (bc) is maximized where marginal benefit (MSV) equals marginal (MSC) cost.*[11] The guidance of the Principle of Maximum Social Gain is therefore summarized in the equality of *MSV* and *MSC*. This principle as applied to the size of the public sector can be stated as follows:

> *Spending by the public sector should be pushed in each area and in total until the marginal social value of the next dollar of expenditure equals the marginal social cost. This will insure that total net gain is maximized.*

C. Model II—Income Transfers and Social Welfare

In this example, the Principle of Maximum Social Gain will be applied to the question of the redistribution of income. Again, some assumptions will be made (rather extreme ones, in this case) and their results will be played out in terms of the principles. First, assume that each citizen in the society gets satisfaction from having income—a rather innocuous proposition. In addition, assume that the relation between each person's income and "social economic welfare" is shown by the social utility of income curve (*SUI*) in Figure 4-4.[12] Finally, assume that there are two people in a society—one whose income level is at *A* (Mr. X) and another whose income level is at *B* (Mr. Y).

Confronted now with the desire to maximize the society's economic welfare through adherence to the Principle of Maximum Social Gain, the government must decide if it is worthwhile to transfer some income from Mr. X to Mr. Y or vice versa. Given the *SUI* curve of Figure 4-4 and the basic principle, the policy conclusion is clear. Money should be transferred from Mr. Y to Mr. X until the last dollar taken from Mr. Y entails a loss of social

---

[11] If this relationship between the total and marginal curves is not familiar to the reader, he should consult the microeconomic theory section of an elementary economics textbook. See, for example, Robert Haveman and Kenyon Knopf, *The Market System*, in this series.

[12] The shape of this curve assumes that a $1 increment to the income of a poor man adds more to society's welfare than if he were a millionaire.

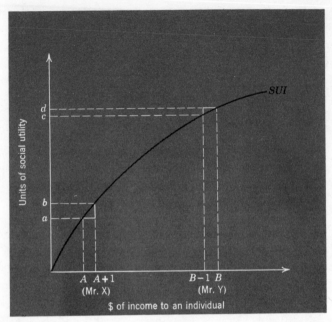

Figure 4-4

utility equal to the gain in social economic welfare from giving it to Mr. X.

From the diagram the logic of this conclusion is clear. The first dollar taken from Mr. Y entails a social welfare loss of *cd*, but giving it to Mr. X provides a social welfare gain of *ab*. Because *ab* > *cd*, the transfer is a worthwhile one. Moreover, dollars should continue to be shifted until the last dollar given up by Mr. Y entails a loss of social utility just equal to that gained by giving it to Mr. X.[13]

[13] The astute reader will not have missed the final result of this overly simple model. When all of the transfers have been accomplished, there will be complete income equality. It should be emphasized that the purpose of this exercise was not to argue for this position. Rather, it was to derive the results of applying the Principle of Maximum Social Gain to a contrived situation based on quite unrealistic assumptions. Obviously, the actual determination of the optimal distribution of society's income must take into consideration many factors which we have assumed away. One of the obvious considerations is the effect of government income redistribution schemes on the level of individual initiative.

It should also be noted that it is not necessary to rely on the awkward

Having then made a social equity judgment (which is embodied in the *SUI* curve), the application of the Principle of Maximum Social Gain to the question of income redistribution leads to the conclusion that:

> *To maximize social utility, dollars of income should be shifted from those people for whom additional income has a low social utility to those for whom additional income has a high social utility until the marginal social utility of income of all people is made equal.*

D. *The Principle of Maximum Social Gain—Revisited*

These examples have clarified the implications of universally applying the Principle of Maximum Social Gain to public sector decisions. The universal application of the principle to government can be summarized in the following three propositions which deal, respectively, with the size of the public sector, the composition of spending, and the composition of taxes.

How much spending should the public sector undertake?

1. The government should continue taxing and spending until the social utility produced by the next dollar spent just equals the social disutility caused by diverting that dollar from the private sector through taxes.

On what programs should the government spend and how much should be spent on each?

2. The government should allocate its spending among programs so that the social utility of the last dollar spent on each program is equal to the social utility of the last dollar spent on every other program.

What types of taxes should the government impose and how much revenue should be raised from each?

social utility of income curve notion in order to discuss the economics of income redistribution. Recently, it was shown that redistribution can be meaningfully discussed using more basic and less unrealistic assumptions than those used here. All that is necessary is to assume that higher income people get satisfaction out of contributing to increasing the incomes of poorer people. See H. M. Hochman and J. D. Rodgers, "Pareto Optimal Redistribution," *American Economic Review* (LIX, Sept. 1969), p. 542.

3. The government should allocate the money which it has to raise among the various forms of taxation so that the social *dis*utility of the last dollar raised from each kind of tax is equal to the social *disutility* of the last dollar raised from every other kind of tax.[14]

Should a government find itself "out of kilter" in any one of these three areas, it could increase the community's well-being by adjusting its size, its spending, or its taxing until the relevant equality was again achieved.

IV. SUMMARY AND CONCLUSIONS

Throughout this discussion of the Principle of Maximum Social Gain, the key notions have been social benefits and costs, social utilities and disutilities, social advantages and disadvantages, and social gains and losses. As applied to the public sector, the principle views taxes as entailing social costs and expenditures as conferring social benefits. Public decisions consistent with the principle entail a balancing of these costs and gains at all of the relevant margins. This is true of exhaustive expenditures as well as income transfer programs. Moreover, both economic efficiency and equity impacts must be considered in evaluating social costs and gains.

[14] These same rules were stated with somewhat more elegance by Sir Hugh Dalton nearly 50 years ago: "Public expenditure . . . should be carried just so far, that the advantage to the community of a further small increase . . . is just counterbalanced by the disadvantage of a correspondingly small increase in taxation . . . . A public authority, not being a person except in a legal sense, cannot estimate the marginal utilities of its various expenditures as an individual can. But the general principle, on which statesmen should attempt to act, is the same. The marginal utility *to the community* of all forms of public expenditure should be equal. The ideal distribution of . . . total public income between different taxes [is] . . . given by the requirement that the marginal social disadvantages, or disutilities, of raising income from all these sources should be equal" (*Principles of Public Finance*, New York: Augustus Kelley, Inc., London: Routledge and Kegan Paul, 1922, p. 14.

5

The Economic Effects of Public Decisions—
Social Gains and Costs

Application of the Principle of Maximum Social Gain requires a careful accounting of both the good things (economic gains) and the bad things (economic losses) which are generated by a public decision. While the meaning of this principle has been discussed, we have given few clues concerning the anatomy of the gains and costs entailed by a public decision.

In this chapter we shall examine the process by which these gains and costs are generated and then dispersed throughout the economy and, in so doing, we shall begin to fill in the analytical framework of the Principle of Maximum Social Gain.

I. THE SOCIAL COSTS OF PUBLIC DECISIONS

As we have seen, government expenditure decisions require that revenue be raised from the private sector, primarily through taxes. The collection of taxes clearly imposes costs on the private sector —by ceding some of their income, taxpayers forego benefits which they could have realized had they been able to spend their income freely. Because of taxes, cars are not purchased (and, hence, not produced) which otherwise would have been, houses are not built which otherwise would have been, factories are not constructed which otherwise would have been, movies are not seen (or made) which otherwise would have been. The social cost of taxes to the private sector, therefore, is the loss of the opportunity to produce, consume, and enjoy some goods and services. To determine the cost of taxes, then, we have to search for these lost opportunities and find out how much they are worth.

To further clarify this statement, the total impact of taxes can be separated into two categories: the *economic efficiency* impact and the *equity* (or income distribution) impact. Each of these effects must be looked at carefully but, first, let us discuss some rudimentary notions and make some basic distinctions.

A. *Direct Taxes and Indirect*

The direct-indirect distinction is the most basic way to distinguish among taxes. When a person on whom a tax is levied truly pays the tax himself, it is a direct tax. In the case of indirect taxes, it is possible for the person who is legally taxed to escape payment by passing the tax on to someone else. These people then end up paying the tax, but indirectly. This kind of shift can often be accomplished if the person legally taxed is a seller who can include the tax in the price of what he sells, thus forcing the buyer to pay it.

The personal income tax is a direct tax—it is very difficult to pass it to someone else. On the other hand, the property tax may be an indirect tax, especially if the property is rental property. In this case, the landlord may be able to shift the tax to his tenant by means of an increase in rent.

B. *Tax Incidence and Burden*

The incidence of a tax, whether direct or indirect, refers to the final source of the tax payment. The person who ultimately sacrifices when a tax is collected is said to bear the tax *burden*. Therefore the location of the tax burden determines the tax incidence.

While, by definition, the location of the burden of a tax defines its incidence, it should be noted that the *real* burden of a tax (of, say, $100) may vary, depending on who is being taxed. If the incidence of a $100 tax falls on a very rich man, its real burden is likely to be smaller than if it falls on a very poor man.[1]

---

[1] This is true even though the monetary burden of the tax is the same in each case—$100.

C. *Types of Taxes*

Although one can distinguish a multitude of various taxes, there is a limited number of the most basic varieties. We shall concentrate here on income, property, inheritance, and commodity taxes. In forming a judgment on the overall structure of taxation in a society, the entire bundle of taxes must be considered and the costs and gains of each type weighed.

In most modern, relatively affluent societies, the backbone of the tax structure is the *income tax*. As its title suggests, this form of tax relates the amount paid by a person in taxes to the amount of his income. In the United States the "persons" on whom income taxes are levied are both individuals and corporations—both individual income earners and profitable corporations are required to pay some proportion of their income to the public sector.

A few characteristics of income-type taxes should be noted. First, with few exceptions, the personal income tax is a direct tax. On the other hand, the incidence of the income tax levied on corporations is not nearly so obvious. The extent to which the corporation income tax can be shifted either to workers in the form of lower wages or to those who purchase the company's products in the form of higher prices is a much-debated issue. Second, the thing which is being taxed in these two kinds of income tax should be specifically noted. In the case of the tax on individuals, it is both the efforts of an individual in earning income and the productivity of his wealth which are being taxed—the more a man works and the more property income he receives, the more taxes he has to pay. In the case of the income tax on corporations, it is the success of the corporation which is the object of taxation. The greater the profits of the business, the more it is required to pay in taxes.

The final important thing to note about the income tax is related to the concept of the progressivity of the tax. Three categories are possible: proportional taxation, regressive taxation, and progressive taxation. A particular income tax structure can possess any of these degrees of progressivity and may possess all three at different levels of income. Under a proportional income tax, a person pays the same proportion of his income in income tax (say, 10 percent) irrespective of his income level. Under regressive taxation, the proportion of a person's income paid in taxes falls as his income rises; under progressive taxation, the proportion rises as income rises. These three categories are exemplified by the curves shown in Figure 5-1.

A second important tax is the levy placed on the ownership of immobile objects; houses, buildings, and land. This tax, commonly called the *property tax*, penalizes individuals for having title to a piece of real property—at least to the extent that the tax is a direct tax. If the incidence of the property tax can be shifted (say, to the renters of property in the form of higher rents), it becomes an indirect tax and fails to impose a penalty on the ownership of real property. In this case, the tax penalizes the occupying of rental property.

The third prominent form of tax is the *inheritance tax*. In an inheritance tax the public sector takes a certain proportion of the estate of a deceased person before it is bequeathed to the deceased person's heirs. The rules which establish how much of the

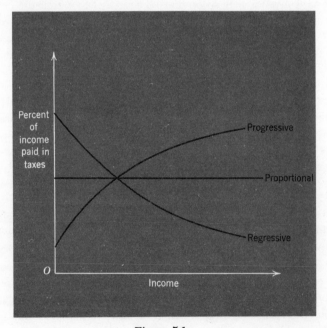

Figure 5-1

estate goes to the government are complicated and, in some cases, prolonged court proceedings are necessary. Because "dead men pay no taxes," the incidence of the inheritance tax falls on the heirs to the estate. Moreover, the heirs cannot shift the burden of the tax to someone else. It is, therefore, a direct tax.

Because the heirs are, in essence, being forced to cede a portion of something they did not possess prior to the death of the person making the bequest, an inheritance tax is generally believed to entail less "pain" than an equivalent tax on, say, income. The similarity of an inheritance tax to a property tax should likewise not go unnoticed. In a sense, an inheritance tax is a special form of property tax. The primary difference is that while property taxes are levied annually, the inheritance tax is levied once and for all at the death of the property owner.

The final category is the *commodity tax.* In most societies, commodity taxes are an important source of public revenue. Common forms of the commodity tax are sales and excise taxes. In the United States, for example, nearly every state government raises revenue by taxing the buying and selling of goods at retail. The national government imposes special excise taxes on those who buy and sell certain commodities, such as liquor, beer, tobacco products, and gasoline.[2]

While commodity taxes are imposed on particular transactions and are typically collected by the government from the seller, it is recognized that the incidence of the tax falls on both the buyer and the seller. For example, even though the tax on alcoholic beverages is collected from the storekeeper who sells them, the buyer pays some of the tax through an increase in liquor prices. Because the seller is able to shift a part of the incidence of this tax onto the buyer, commodity taxes are generally regarded as indirect taxes.

Commodity taxes can be differentiated in two ways. Some commodity taxes are general; others are particular. Some commodity taxes are *ad valorem*; others are specific. The distinction between general and particular taxes hinges on the extent to which the coverage of a tax hits all commodities at a particular level of trade

[2] It is not widely known that the federal government levies a $200 excise tax on the sale of machine guns. There is a precedent for gun control legislation!

or whether it is levied on only certain commodities. Most retail sales taxes are general in that all commodities sold by retailers are covered. Often, however, there are particular commodities on which special taxes are levied. In the United States, alcohol, tobacco, and gasoline receive such special treatment.

The distinction between *ad valorem* and specific taxes hinges on which characteristic of a commodity is subject to the tax. A physical characteristic of the commodity is the basis for computing a specific tax. The size of an *ad valorem* commodity tax depends on the value or price of the commodity. Hence, a 3 percent sales tax is an *ad valorem* tax; 3¢ is collected on a $1 tie, 6¢ is collected on a $2 tie. An example of a specific tax would be a $1 tax on each case of beer sold, or a 10¢ tax collected on each theater ticket sold.

Like income and property taxes, commodity taxes are either progressive or regressive, depending on how big a chunk of a person's income they absorb relative to the size of that income. For example, a general retail sales tax tends to be regressive because poor people spend a higher proportion of their income on purchasing commodities and services at retail than do rich people. Similarly, particular taxes on various kinds of luxury goods—for example, furs, long-distance telephone calls, and jewelry—tend to be progressive taxes because such goods are purchased mainly by the wealthy. Because the wealthy usually buy more expensive goods than the poor, *ad valorem* taxes tend to be less regressive (more progressive) than specific commodity taxes.

D. *The Economic Efficiency Impact of Taxes*

In Chapter 2, the operation of a smoothly functioning market system was described. It was pointed out that the system would answer the questions of what, how, and for whom in line with the tastes and preferences of the people of the society, insofar as these tastes and preferences were backed up by a willingness to pay. We argued that except for certain market failures (noted in Chapter 3), the market system would get the "right" goods produced and would get them produced in the most effective or efficient way. Stated another way, aside from market failures, the market system generates the optimum *size* GNP as well as its optimum *composition*.

The imposition of taxes can affect both the size and the make-up of a nation's GNP. To the extent that both the size and composition of GNP were ideal prior to the levying of taxes, the imposition of taxes is likely to alter these variables so as to reduce society's economic welfare.[3] The size of GNP is likely to be smaller and its composition less to society's liking.

To demonstrate how taxes can decrease the economic welfare of society, we shall study two cases. In the first case, we shall analyze how the income tax might affect the *size* of the national income (GNP). In the second case, the effect of a commodity tax on the *composition* of GNP will be presented.

1. *Case I—The Income Tax and the Size of GNP.* After stripping away many of the complications and reservations from the economic theory which explains the size and growth of a nation's GNP, one is left with a very simple statement.

> Given a certain level of technology, GNP and its growth depend on *both* the productive effort which the people of a society expend and the resources which they devote to the production of investment (rather than consumption) goods.

The larger the productive effort expended and the larger the level of investment, the larger will be a nation's GNP and the faster it will grow. This can be stated symbolically as follows:

$$\text{GNP} = f\,(E, I).$$

GNP is a function of (depends on) productive effort (E) and the level of investment (I).

While E and I directly determine the level and growth of GNP, they, in turn, are determined by other variables. Again, stripping theory to its bare bones, we can say that:

> The productive effort expended in a society (E) depends on the *ability* of a people to expend effort (A_e) and their *desire* or willingness to expend it (D_e).

> Similarly, the level of investment in a society (I) depends on the *ability* of the citizens to invest (A_i) and their *desire* to invest (D_i).

[3] It should be noted that we are concerned here *only* with the imposition of taxes, not with a joint expenditure-tax package.

We can write:

$$E = f\ (A_e, D_e),$$
$$I = f\ (A_i, D_i).$$

It is through affecting the *abilities* (A_e, A_i) and *desires* (D_e, D_i) of the people of a society that the imposition of, say, an income tax can alter the size of a nation's GNP.

Consider first how the imposition of an income tax could affect the ability of a society to expend productive effort (A_e). While the linkages between the imposition of a tax and the ability to work are many and complicated, one stands out. Without question, up to a certain point the better a man's diet and the more congenial his surroundings, the more productive will be his work. Indeed, poor people are often ineffective workers because they are poor and ill-fed and, in turn, they are poor and ill-fed because they are ineffective workers—a vicious cycle. To the extent that an income tax requires payments from people at the lower end of the income distribution, it reduces their effectiveness as productive workers; the tax reduces their ability to work (A_e) and, hence, tends to decrease GNP.[4]

An income tax is also likely to affect the ability of the society to invest (A_i). When a society invests part of its annual production in machines, factories, and other capital goods, it is fostering economic growth. These capital goods increase the productivity of the labor which works with them and enables GNP in future years to be larger than it otherwise would be. However, to undertake investment, a society has to divert some of its spending from the purchase of consumption goods (food, clothes, and theater tickets) to provide for the future—the purchase of investment goods.

What will happen now if an income tax is levied? In all likelihood, the imposition of such a tax will force a reduction in both consumption and investment. By siphoning off some of society's spending power, there is less "disposable income" remaining for either ice cream (consumption) or a new piece of equipment (investment). Because a lower level of investment implies a lower

---

[4] It is interesting to note that one of the major reforms in the tax reform effort of 1969 was to exempt income earners in the poverty category from the payment of personal income taxes.

rate of growth of GNP, the income tax has a negative effect on economic welfare through the A_i variable as well as the A_e variable.

The effect of the tax on the "desire variables" (D_e and D_i) works through a more complicated set of relationships about which we know relatively little. The reason for this stems from the fact that the desires both to expend productive effort (D_e) and to invest (D_i) are tied up with the incentives which motivate humans. Are people willing to expend more units of effort if they are paid \$2 per hour than if they are paid \$1.75 per hour, or are they not? Does a higher expected profit rate lead people to risk more or less of their resources on an investment in a new plant which may turn out either better or worse than expected? These are the kinds of questions which must be answered in dealing with the impact of an income tax on D_e and D_i—and the answers are not clear.

Figure 5-2 is helpful in thinking about these questions. On the

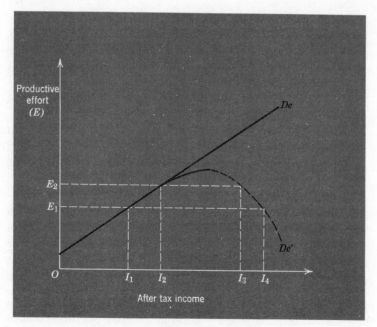

Figure 5-2

horizontal axis of that figure a person's income after taxes is plotted. The expenditure of productive effort (E) is plotted on the vertical axis. The curve labeled D_e shows how this person's willingness to work is related to the income which he gets to keep. The D_e curve says that the person is willing to expend more effort as his after-tax income goes up. At income level I_1, he will expend E_1 units of effort; at income level I_2, he will increase the amount of effort to E_2. This fits the traditional notion that to increase someone's pay encourages him to work harder. If this kind of incentive does exist, the effect on GNP of imposing an income tax is clear. To introduce a tax on people's income reduces their willingness to expend as much effort as they had previously. The tax, therefore, has a negative effect on GNP. As people's disposable income is reduced through taxes, they expend less productive effort, and GNP goes down.

However, it is not clear that the curve looks like D_e. It may look like D'_e. That is, it may be positively sloped at low levels of income (like D_e) and negatively sloped at high income levels (like the dotted line). For example, higher income people may get used to a certain standard of affluence so that, if an income tax is imposed, they may increase the amount they work in an attempt to maintain that level of living. A tax bite which reduces their "disposable" income from I_4 to I_3 will in this case expand productive effort from E_1 to E_2. With this sort of behavior, the effect of the tax on GNP will be positive—the lowered disposable income will bring forth more productive effort and, hence, raise GNP.[5]

While most people believe that the pertinent curve looks like D_e and not D'_e, the best economic analysis of this matter has concluded:

[5] One of the reasons the influence of taxes on work effort may not be negative has to do with that oft-noted human trait called "conspicuous consumption." Sir Hugh Dalton described this effect as follows. "There are many who desire not merely to be well-off, but to be visibly better-off than those whom they regard as their social rivals. Hence, . . . springs that ostentatious *extravagance*, typified by the story told of Carnegie, who kept four chauffeurs, because Astor, who lived just across the road, kept only three. The desire to work and save, in order to indulge a sense of vainglorious vanity is not likely to be much, if at all, abated by increased taxation." *Principles of Public Finance, op. cit.*, pp. 76-77.

The point of view that high income tax rates . . . seriously sap the work incentives of . . . people and thereby deter economic growth has been presented with great vigor and persistence. Typically, the conclusion is treated as self-evident . . . . [However,] . . . there are at least as good reasons for believing that . . . taxation will have a net incentive effect as there are for believing it will have a disincentive effect.[6]

The analysis of the impact of an income tax on the desire to invest (D_i) closely parallels the analysis of the relationship between an income tax and the willingness of people to expend productive effort. There are a number of reasons to expect the level of investment to fall when taxes absorb part of a firm's profit. For one thing, business investment tends to be financed out of retained earnings—profits not paid out in dividends. On the other hand, there are reasons to expect a tax increase to generate an increase in investment under certain circumstances. For example, the tax may represent a commitment of government to control an inflation which was undermining investor's confidence. In general, however, it is believed that a tax will have a discouraging effect on investment. It is reasonable to assume that investment and, therefore, GNP will decrease when an income tax is imposed on business income where one previously did not exist.

From this analysis of the variables which influence the level of a nation's economic activity (A_i, A_e, D_i, D_e), it seems likely that the imposition of taxes or the alteration of their level does influence the GNP of a nation, the economic welfare of its people, and the economic efficiency of its market system. In particular, the economic linkages discussed above argue that the imposition of a tax on income will *reduce* the level of output of an economy from its previous level. This result is summarized in Figure 5-3. In the figure the arrows express the linkages between the variables and the signs summarize the likely direction of these relationships.

Case II—Commodity Taxes and the Composition of GNP. Economic efficiency is concerned with the makeup of a society's total output as well as its size. While Case I focused on the process by

[6] George F. Break, "The Effects of Taxation on Work Incentives," *Federal Tax Policy for Economic Growth and Stability,* Joint Economic Committee, 1955, p. 192.

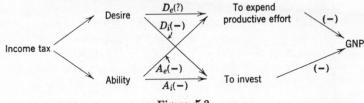

Figure 5-3

which taxes influenced the size of GNP, this case will deal with the relationship of taxes to the composition of GNP. As we have seen, aside from "market failures," the logic of economics gives a basis for expecting the basket of goods and services turned out by an unobstructed market system to be, in some sense, optimum. Consequently, if the imposition of taxes alters this pattern, it can be argued that the efficiency of the economy in meeting the desires of consumers has been reduced.

The efficiency of the market system in getting the "right" amounts of the "right" things produced is illustrated by the standard supply and demand diagram of Figure 5-4. The competitive market price, P, equates the value of the last unit bought, as seen by the buyer, with the cost of getting that unit produced. It would cost more to produce the next unit beyond X_1 than it would be worth; if production stopped before X_1, additional units could be produced whose value is greater than the cost of their production. Output X_1 is, therefore, the "right" output.

The question is: Does the imposition of a tax affect the quantity of a good which is produced and sold? Does it disturb the free market equilibrium? To analyze this question a specific commodity tax will be employed: a tax levied on, say, the seller of eyeglasses, of X per pair of glasses sold.

As we have seen, a specific commodity tax is a penalty which the government imposes on the seller of a good (or service) for the production and sale of the good. To the seller, the tax is just like a cost which has to be met on each unit which he sells. If, for example, the tax on eyeglasses is $2 per pair, the costs of the businessman are increased by $2 for each pair of glasses sold. The relationship of this statement to Figure 5-4 now becomes clear. Because the supply curve of that figure is a picture of the marginal costs of the sellers of the product, the imposition of a

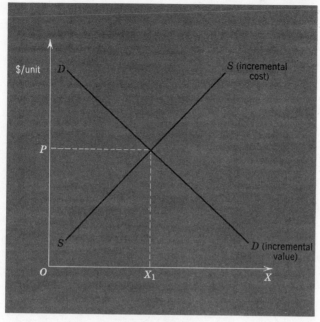

Figure 5-4

per unit sales tax modifies the level of that curve. Indeed, the imposition of a $2 excise tax on eyeglasses raises the marginal cost of producing and selling one more pair. This effect is shown in Figure 5-5.

Because of the tax, the supply (marginal cost) curve is shifted upward by $2 per unit from S to S'. It is as if an additional cost of $2 per pair had to be met by the seller of eyeglasses. This imposition of the tax is bound to affect the market price and the quantity exchanged—as a penalty on "supplying," the tax cannot help but modify the equilibrium. While the before-tax equilibrium was at E representing X_1 units sold at a price of P_1, the tax, by raising the supply curve, generates a new equilibrium at E'. This represents an increase in price from P_1 to P_2 and a decrease in the quantity exchanged from X_1 to X_2.[7]

---

[7] From Figure 5-5, the short-run *incidence* of commodity taxes can also be analyzed. Because the effect of the tax is to raise the price, it is clear that buyers indirectly pay some of the tax. In the diagram of Figure 5-5, the

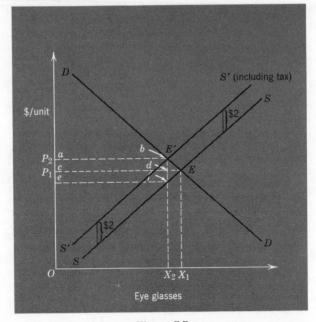

Figure 5-5

From the information conveyed by this modified equilibrium, it is clear that taxes do, indeed, affect the composition of an economy's output. In particular, the impact of sales, excise, or other commodity taxes is to raise the price of the commodity on which they are imposed and to reduce the quantity which gets produced and exchanged. By altering the free market equilibrium, such taxes decrease the economic efficiency of a market system. They lead to an allocation of resources and pattern of output which is different from that which would result from the freely expressed demands of buyers interacting with the costs of sellers. Less is produced and exchanged of those goods on which the tax

total tax bill is *abfe* ($2 times OX_2). Of that tax bill, buyers pay *abdc* and sellers pay *cdfe*. The reader would do well to think through this result on his own. With slightly more thought it can be seen that the division of the tax between buyer and seller depends on the elasticity of the supply and demand curves. Indeed, the tax is shared between buyer and seller in the ratio of the elasticity of supply over the elasticity of demand. *Hint*: Try a demand (supply) curve that is infinitely elastic.

is imposed; consequently, relatively more of other goods is produced.

The imposition of taxes, then, affects the economic efficiency of the economy by influencing both the *size* and the *composition* of the nation's final output. Because the GNP tends to be smaller and its composition less than optimum, taxes impose a real cost on the society. Those taxes which adversely affect the ability and desire to work, produce, and invest reduce the nation's GNP. The primary kinds of taxes with this impact are income and commodity taxes. Taxes that penalize the production of certain goods also reduce the allocative efficiency of the market system. The prime culprits here are the sales and excise (commodity) taxes. In general, inheritance and property taxes are among the most neutral (least harmful) in their impact on the efficiency with which the market system allocates the society's resources and produces the products consumers most desire.

E. *The Equity (or Income Distribution) Impact of Taxes*

While public sector decisions on taxation affect the quantity and composition of production in an economy, they even more clearly affect the way society's income is distributed among its people. Indeed, taxation policy is a very important tool by which the government achieves the degree of income equality (or inequality) which it deems appropriate. In this section we shall explore just two topics in the larger question of the impact of taxes on the distribution of society's income. First, the implication for tax policy of a particular, but rather widely accepted, judgment on the relationship of income to people's economic welfare will be explored. Second, the impact of the most common types of taxes on income distribution will be analyzed. The first of these topics deals with the question of what the structure of taxes *should* be if it is premised on the particular value judgment we shall describe. The second deals with the actual distributional effects of different taxes; it deals with a question of fact and, hence, requires no prior value judgment.

If we accept that a certain amount of taxes must be levied by a government which adheres to the Principle of Maximum Social Gain, it follows that the government must seek to raise that revenue by imposing the least burden possible on the society.

However, to speak about the burden of raising a certain amount of taxes, one must know how much economic welfare people get from their income or, alternatively, how much satisfaction people lose when they are forced to sacrifice some of their income. It has often been argued that the relationship between a man's economic well-being (or utility) and his income is pictured by a curve of the shape of *TU* in Figure 5-6. This curve shows that total utility rises as income goes up, but that it rises at a decreasing rate. Consequently, the *TU* curve of Figure 5-6 slopes upward but becomes increasingly flat. When a man is poor, an *additional* dollar means a great deal to him; when he becomes rich, one more dollar confers less additional utility than when he was poor. The shape of this curve embodies the Principle of Diminishing Marginal Utility of Income.

If it is accepted that all people in a society are similar in the amount of economic welfare gained from income, and that these separate economic welfares can be meaningfully aggregated,[8] it follows that, in order to keep the pain of taxes small, the system of taxation should be a progressive one. This is so because a dollar of income taken from a rich person implies a smaller loss of satisfaction than a dollar taken from a poor person. Even if it is required that all income earners in society contribute to the tax bill, these assumptions demand progressivity in the tax structure —that is, if the government is to minimize the loss of economic welfare caused by its tax system.

If the utility of income is as we have assumed, it is relatively

[8] Joan Robinson, a famous British economist, stated the following about assumptions like these. "To a strictly logical mind any discussion of utility to more than one individual is repugnant. It is not really justifiable to talk about maximum satisfaction to a whole population. But common sense protests that if we treat all individuals as being exactly alike, it is then permissable to sum their satisfactions, and that human beings, in their economic needs, are sufficiently alike to make the discussion of aggregate satisfaction interesting. Upon this basis we may say that if any two individuals have the same real income they derive the same satisfaction from it. We may further say that if one individual has a larger real income than another the marginal utility of income to him is less." Joan Robinson, *The Economics of Imperfect Competition* (London: MacMillan and Co., 1933), p. 318. Reprinted by permission of the publisher. It should be noted, however, that many contemporary theorists conclude that this sort of addition of satisfaction has no analytical meaning. See note 13 of Chapter 4 for a further discussion of this matter.

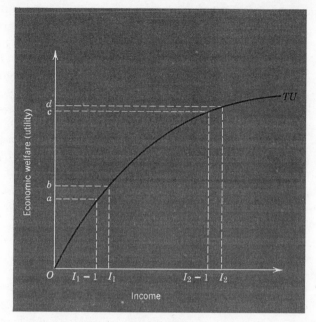

Figure 5-6

easy to show that rich people should sacrifice a larger proportion of their income than poor people to reduce the social cost of taxes to a low level. In Figure 5-6, a typical poor person's income is plotted at I_1 and a rich person's income is plotted at I_2. By taking a dollar away from each, the rich man is moved to I_2-1 and the poor man is shifted to I_1-1. From the total utility of income curve (TU), it is seen that the loss of utility from $1 of taxes to the poor man (ab) is substantially larger than the utility loss to the rich man (cd). It does not take a giant leap to argue from this that rich people ought to contribute a greater proportion of their income to the tax bill than should poor—if taxes are to be raised with the lowest feasible loss of economic welfare.[9]

[9] While this argument provides a logic for defending progressive taxation, many past proponents of progressivity have not found it necessary to resort to the Principle of Diminishing Marginal Utility of Income. For many, the simple judgment that taxes should be used as a tool to secure equity, to reduce the inequality of incomes, has been sufficient. As a former British Chancellor of the Exchequer put it: "The plain man can favour progressive taxation simply on the ground that, as it seems to him, it reduces inequality."

Different kinds of taxes have different effects on the distribution of income. Some are progressive, others neutral, and still others regressive. Some taxes can be structured so as to make them either progressive or regressive. The *income tax* is of this latter variety. While income taxes in nearly all countries have been designed to take a larger portion of the rich man's income than of the poor man's, they do not necessarily have to do this. It requires no technical sleight-of-hand to place the burden of the income tax on the poor man; only legislation with higher tax rates applied to low rather than high incomes would be needed.

On the other hand, *inheritance taxes* are, nearly without exception, progressive. One has to have something of value to bequeath before it can be taxed. In addition, most countries have structured this tax so that it takes a bigger bite out of larger bequeathals than of smaller. For similar reasons, the *property tax* also tends to be naturally progressive. It is the wealthy who are the primary owners of property in a society.

In the category of naturally regressive taxes, one finds the largely obsolete, but once quite popular, *poll tax*. In the United States, this tax has been associated primarily with the levy of a fixed number of dollars on all people who vote. As such, this tax requires a higher proportion of the income of the poor than of the rich—the definition of regressivity.[10] Finally, as we noted earlier, most *commodity taxes* tend to be regressive. For example, because poor people spend a higher proportion of their income on retail purchases than do the rich, sales taxes take a proportionately bigger bite of the income of the poor than of the well-to-do.

II. THE SOCIAL GAINS OF PUBLIC DECISIONS

In much the same way that taxes impose costs on the private economy, government spending confers gains. In our discussion of the social costs of taxation, we have done much of the spadework necessary for understanding how public expenditures generate welfare gains.

---

[10] The use of the poll tax as a prerequisite to voting was widely used in the southern states prior to its being outlawed by Constitutional amendment in 1964. As a simple head tax, however, the poll tax is still found in the United States—for example, Cambridge, Massachusetts still employs such a tax.

Just as it was necessary to differentiate the different types of taxes, we must distinguish among expenditure categories. The most basic distinction is that between *exhaustive* and *nonexhaustive* expenditures. While nonexhaustive expenditures take the form of outright grants of money to private citizens or private businesses, exhaustive expenditures refer to government purchases of goods and services. Nonexhaustive, or *transfer,* expenditures are therefore exactly the converse of taxes. Instead of money going from private citizens to the government, the process is simply reversed. In the United States, social security benefits, unemployment compensation, and veterans' benefits are examples of these nonexhaustive expenditures.

A. *Transfer Expenditures*

Because they are direct payments, analysis of the impact of transfer expenditures requires the same set of concepts we used to think about the effect of taxes on the economy. For example, like taxes, some transfer expenditures are *direct* (social security benefits), while others are *indirect* (subsidy payments to the airlines). In the case of direct transfers, the gains accrue to the person receiving the payment; for indirect transfers the incidence or impact may be shifted to other people. For example, in the case of airline subsidies, some people may benefit in addition to airline owners. If the subsidy induces airlines to charge lower fares than they otherwise would have, airline passengers will reap some of the gain.

Transfer expenditures, like taxes, can be *progressive, regressive,* or *neutral.* In this case it is the proportion of the recipient's income that is made up of the transfer which determines the presence or absence of progressivity. If the transfer composes a larger proportion of the income of the poor than it does of the rich, it is progressive; if not, it is either neutral or regressive. It is on this basis that social security benefits are judged to be progressive as, to be sure, are welfare and aid-to-dependent-children payments. Again, the Principle of Diminishing Marginal Utility of Income, if accepted, can provide the basis for defending a progressive structure of transfer-type public expenditures.

It is important to recognize that nonexhaustive or transfer expenditures have economic efficiency impacts as well as redistributional or equity impacts. Like taxes, they can alter the size of the society's GNP or its composition, or both. In analyzing these efficiency impacts, the framework developed earlier with respect to taxes must again be used. How does a transfer payment affect the ability and desire to expend productive effort (A_e and D_e)? How does a transfer expenditure affect the ability and desire to invest (A_i and D_i)? To analyze the impact of particular non-exhaustive expenditures on the *size* of the GNP requires a tracing of the impact of the transfers on the variables which determine the level of the GNP; namely, D_e, A_e, A_i, and D_i. In Figure 5-3 we have summarized how changes in these variables affect the level of GNP.

Indirect transfers (such as per unit subsidies to businesses who sell certain products, like airplane rides) affect the *composition* of GNP through the same set of relationships as do commodity taxes. Again, one must analyze the effect of the transfer on marginal costs (see Figure 5-5) to discover how the composition of the nation's output will be affected. Whereas commodity taxes raise marginal costs and shift supply curves to the left, per unit subsidies reduce marginal costs and increase supply curves. The subsidy, therefore, generates the opposite output effects from the commodity tax.

B. Exhaustive Expenditures

To evaluate the impact of *exhaustive* public expenditures on the economy requires a substantially different framework than we used in evaluating transfer expenditures. In undertaking exhaustive expenditures, a government plays much the same role as a business. It buys resources (land, labor, capital) or commodities from the private sector using its tax revenues for payment; it transforms the things it purchases into public outputs valued by citizens; and finally, it either sells these outputs to private citizens or gives them away. Contemporary examples of exhaustive expenditures are education, national defense, electricity, roads, postal services, job training, market information, flood protection, flights into space, housing, national parks, and libraries.[11]

[11] It is a good exercise to determine how the United States government disposes of the services of these public outputs. Which ones does it give

It will be recalled that the public sector performs these economic functions because spillovers or other market failures either keep private industry from producing the commodity or cause it to produce the commodity in the "wrong" amounts. Because these exhaustive expenditures involve the production of an output by the government, the model which we used to form a judgment of the "goodness" or "badness" of private sector production can be used here as well. Again the question must be: Are the right things being produced by the government and in the right quantities?

In answering this question for the public sector, we must again focus on the costs and gains of decisions. Presuming that the goal of the public sector is to satisfy the preferences and desires of the citizens—the same test which we required of private sector decisions—the familiar notions of willingness-to-pay (demand) and cost are again relevant. Take, as an example, the public sector's provision of job-training services as represented in Figure 5-7.

The first question which must be answered in discussing the government's provision of job-training services is: What is the willingness of people to pay for the "outputs" generated by job training? If job-training services are provided, the incomes of trained workers will tend to go up—and they would be willing to pay something for that. The productivity of laborers will go up, meaning that business will likely earn more net profits—and they would be willing to pay something for that. The prices of the goods which these trained workers produce may fall because of their increased productivity—and consumers would be prepared to pay something for that. These retrained workers may be able to move out of the ghetto, decreasing their contribution to the social costs of that situation—and society as a whole would be willing to pay something for that. All of these willingnesses to pay are incorporated into the total social benefit (*TSB*) curve shown in Figure 5-7.

The second question to be asked pertains to the costs to society of providing this training service. Teachers must be hired, space

away? For which outputs does it require a payment—in the fashion of private business?

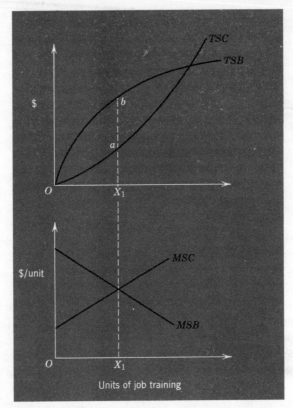

Figure 5-7

for the training center must be provided, the workers must be pulled off their existing jobs (thus decreasing their current contribution to society's output) and so on. All of the social costs of providing these job-training services are conceptually summarized in the total social cost (*TSC*) curve of Figure 5-7.[12]

In the lower portion of Figure 5-7, the marginal social cost (*MSC*) and the marginal social benefit (*MSB*) curves are shown. As will be recalled, these incremental curves are uniquely related to the "total" curves and can be located as soon as the "total"

---

[12] It should be stressed that in this analysis cost refers to the total social opportunity costs of the investment and not simply the dollar cost of taxes which has been used previously.

curves are known. The task of the public sector operating according to the Principle of Maximum Social Gain is now clear—provide job-training services until the social gains of the next unit fail to exceed the social costs. This optimum amount of job training is located at X_1 in Figure 5-7.

At output X_1 the difference between *TSB* and *TSC*—*ab*—is maximized. At X_1, marginal social benefit (*MSB*) equals marginal social cost (*MSC*). Hence, X_1 is the "right" amount of job training for the public sector to provide; it is consistent with the Principle of Maximum Social Gain.

In evaluating the effect of an exhaustive public expenditure on the economy, it is this benefit-cost, social gain-social loss test which must be applied. If the gain to society from an expenditure exceeds the cost, the expenditure is an "efficient" one. Such an expenditure is in the public interest and should be undertaken.[13]

It will be noticed that this discussion has revolved around the value of the public output relative to the value of the required inputs. It is this kind of comparison which must be performed to evaluate the impact of the expenditure on the nation's GNP. It is an economic efficiency comparison and, hence, abstracts from equity or income distribution considerations. For example, according to this kind of efficiency comparison, a public project having $400,000 worth of benefits and $399,000 worth of costs would be judged a worthwhile undertaking even if rich people get all the benefits and poor people pay all the costs. However, if equity considerations are relevant, the impact of an exhaustive expenditure on the distribution of income should not be ignored. If dollars of income to poor men are worth more to society than dollars of income to rich men, the way in which the costs and the benefits of an exhaustive expenditure are distributed does make a difference. In Chapter 8, we shall return to this matter.

III. SUMMARY AND CONCLUSIONS

In this chapter, we have analyzed how public decisions impose costs or confer benefits on a society. Costs of public decisions

---

[13] It should be noted that we are assuming here that the effect of such an exhaustive expenditure on the distribution of income is of no acocunt.

were viewed as stemming largely from decisions to levy taxes. Because of taxes, both the size and the composition of the nation's GNP are changed and both changes entail a reduction in the welfare of the people. The ability and desire to work and invest are the crucial links in evaluating the impact of taxes on the *size* of GNP. The modification of the free market output by taxes is the means by which the imposition of taxes affects the *composition* of GNP.

The framework developed for analyzing the effect of taxes on the economy is also helpful in understanding how public expenditures increase the economic welfare of society. Both exhaustive and nonexhaustive expenditures were analyzed.

In this chapter, then, flesh was attached to the bare-bones analytical framework presented in Chapter 4. While that chapter presumed that public decisions have social costs and benefits, this chapter described the nature of these gains and losses and the process by which they get imposed (or conferred) on the people of an economy. Again, we have argued that the Principle of Maximum Social Gain is the basic criterion for evaluating the worth of public taxation and expenditure decisions.

PART FOUR

6

The Federal Budget—Its Construction and Structure

So far in our discussion of public sector economics, we have restricted ourselves to conceptual and analytical issues. We have relied primarily on the logic of economic theory to understand how the market system works and where it fails and why collective action is required when there is market failure. Similarly, the model which we constructed for evaluating the worth of public expenditures and the cost of taxes was based on deductive logic. To this point the concepts of economic efficiency and equity are but theoretical notions.

In both this and succeeding chapters, we leap from theory to the facts. In this chapter the budget of the federal government will be examined. We shall explore its composition, the sources of its revenue, and the objects of its disbursement. In Chapter 7, the structure of the federal government tax system—one side of the federal budget—is analyzed. In Chapter 8, the economics of the expenditure side of the budget is discussed. Chapter 9 relates both sides of the budget in a discussion of the public debt.

I. THE BUDGET-MAKING PROCESS

The formation of the budget of the United States government is a formidable enterprise. It involves, quite literally, thousands of individuals and hundreds of millions of man-hours. To a significant extent the federal establishment and Washington, D.C. revolve around the "budget cycle."

Nearly all of the people involved in the federal government budget-making process are associated with one of four primary "actors." These performers, in order of their appearance, are: the heads of federal agencies, the Bureau of the Budget, the President, and the Congress.

The budget of the federal government, like that of businesses and households, has two sides—revenue and expenditure. However, in any particular year, the budgetary process typically focuses only on the expenditure side. This is so because the tax structure of the government is set by law. As such, it is subject to relatively infrequent alterations. Because the revenue structure is fairly stable, the budget makers in both the executive branch and the Congress have a fairly good notion of how much revenue will be forthcoming from the tax system in the year for which they are forming the budget.

To see how a budget is built, let us take one of the most recent ones on which Congress has acted—the Fiscal Year (FY) 1969 budget, which covered federal government expenditures from July 1, 1968, to June 30, 1969. The inception of the FY 1969 budget occurred in the first months of 1967—over two years before the end of the period which it covered. At this time, individual bureaus and branches of the executive agencies developed an initial FY 1969 plan of the programs for which they are responsible and attempted to identify the likely policy issues pertinent to the budget. This planning was initiated at the request of the Director of the Bureau of the Budget in a letter sent to the Secretaries and other agency heads. This beginning point for the FY 1969 budget cycle is shown in Figure 6-1.

In the budget planning process at the bureau and branch level, bureau chiefs were given a rough target estimate of what they could expect their total budget to be. On the basis of the target figures they developed expenditure estimates of subprogram categories so as to remain within the overall budget constraint. These "first-stab" budget estimates were then submitted by bureau chiefs to the head of the agency.

The agency head and his budget staff, with all of the branch budget estimates in hand, attempted to coordinate these parts in

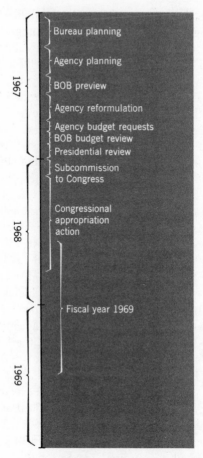

Figure 6-1

order to form the first rough budget estimates for the entire agency. This was done in April and May of 1967—still over a year before the beginning of the period for which the budget was being designed. This initial budget was formed in close cooperation with the component bureaus and branches.

In June the President, working through his executive staff in the Bureau of the Budget, held the *spring preview* of the budget. Agency plans, memoranda, and studies were received by the Bureau of the Budget and comments on and reactions to them were prepared. In this executive preview, policy decisions were made—the budgets of certain agencies and programs were tagged for expansion, others were scheduled for expenditure reductions. By August the budgetary implications of these decisions were conveyed to the agencies. At this time the agency head made additional policy decisions on the basis of information presented by the Bureau of the Budget and his own judgments—some bureau, branch, and program budgets were adjusted downward; others were expanded. Following this, negotiation between the budget staff of the agency and the chiefs of its component bureaus centered on these executive and agency head decisions. This process of negotiation and budget rearrangement was necessary to get agency budget estimates consistent with presidential and departmental policy. It occupied budget officers for most of the summer.

This process was completed in October. At this time, the agencies submitted formal budget requests and final memoranda to the Bureau of the Budget (and, hence, indirectly to the President). For the next month, the professional analysts in the Bureau of the Budget held *budget review* sessions on the agency budget request. At these hearings, agency heads, accompanied by their staffs, defended the structure and size of their budget request against the probings of the Bureau analysts.

When this (hopefully) adversary process was completed and the agency requests modified in line with executive policy, the staff of the Bureau of the Budget assembled all of the component parts for the overall review of the Director. Following his review, the budget was sent to the President for further review. At this stage, the President reappraised (and probably revised) his previously outlined policy decisions and judged the consistency of the budget with these decisions. Following the adjustments resulting from this process, the budget was placed in final form and printed up. All of these final reviews occurred in November and December of 1967 for the FY 1969 budget.

On January 29, 1968, President Johnson submitted to the Congress the five-volume work, *The Budget of the United States, Fiscal Year 1969*, together with his annual budget message which described and defended the size and structure of the budget. This budget, it should be noted, represented only the wishes of the executive branch of the government and the President—it had yet to be funded by the Congress.

With the January budget submission, budget responsibility fell to the Congress. Because the House of Representatives is given primary responsibility for matters of governmental finance, Congressional consideration of the budget started there. It was the House Appropriations Committee that first began legislative action on the proposed budget. This committee has 51 members and is organized into 13 subcommittees, each of which has responsibility for a particular kind of proposed expenditure—agriculture, atomic energy, labor, and so on. Each subcommittee held hearings on the portion of the budget for which it is responsible and developed an appropriations bill containing its recommendations. These bills were then reported to the full committee, which passed them, in some cases making slight modifications. The full committee, in turn, reported the bills to the floor of the House. There they were passed, sometimes only after amendment.

Following House passage, the Senate went through much the same subcommittee-committee-full membership routine. As is inevitable, the appropriations bills passed by the Senate and House differed in both size and structure and, as is usual, the Senate bills were the larger of the two. The differences between the House and Senate versions were resolved by a conference committee made up of a limited number of members of both bodies. With approval of the conference report by both Houses, the appropriation legislation went to the President for his signature.

The process of Congressional consideration of the budget extended over several months. Beginning with the submission of the President's budget in January, the process dragged on into the autumn—well into the fiscal year for which appropriations are made. For the FY 1969 budget, final Congressional action was not completed until October 1968, three months after the beginning of the fiscal year. In this situation, the agencies operated at about the budget level of the previous fiscal year. New program thrusts included in the President's budget were held up until passage of the Appropriation Bill.[1]

[1] In this brief discussion of the budgetary process, we skipped over two matters which should, at least, be mentioned. First, most appropriation bills

From beginning to end, this budgetary cycle lasted about 18 months. Without question, the process is an arduous, involved, and time-consuming one. This having been said, it should be added that its purpose is to enable the built-in checks-and-balances of the government to become operative. The demands of bureaus within an agency tend to be checked by the agency head; agency demands tend to be checked by the President through the Bureau of the Budget; the President tends to be checked by the Congress; and the Congress, with its various interest groups and two Houses, tends to check itself and, in turn, to be checked by the people. Indeed, this bargaining process is precisely what one hopes for from the democratic political structure on which the federal government rests. For this reason, the budget has been referred to as "a political document without equal."

While much more could be said about this budget process, a few points seems worthy of particular comment. First, because of the intricacy, complexity, and length of the process, a long time passes before a newly elected political administration can get its values reflected in the budget. For example, even if the structure of the budget was the first thing the Nixon Administration worked on in January 1969, the first real "Nixon Budget" would be the FY 1971 budget presented to the Congress a year after the beginning of the new administration. This budget would not go into effect until July 1970—and then only if the Congress completes appropriation action by the end of June. This built-in overlap insures that policy changes from one administration to the next will not be radical ones in the U.S. political system.

In addition to this budget lag, there is another factor insuring stability in the federal budget. This is the "uncontrollability" feature of a number of the major budget items, for which the level

cannot be passed by the Congress unless the appropriation has been authorized. The process of authorization of appropriations occurs when a substantive committee of Congress (for example, the Armed Services Committee) reports out a bill authorizing the Congress to appropriate a certain amount for each of a number of items in the budget for which it has jurisdiction (for example, military procurement). Second, even though a particular budget has been passed, there is little to prohibit an agency from returning to the Congress requesting supplemental appropriations. The Supplemental Appropriation Bill follows much the same process as the regular Appropriation Bill.

of expenditure is predetermined by decisions which have already been made. The payment of interest on the national debt, for example, is determined by the borrowing which has taken place in prior years—especially in the World War II period—and the interest rates on outstanding bonds. The federal expenditures in any year for social security benefits are determined by the number of older persons and the benefits which they can claim by law. Once construction on a large capital facility has been started, there is a presumption that construction expenditures will continue until it is completed—sometimes more than a decade. In a recent study of the FY 1969 budget, it was estimated that 48 percent of federal expenditures were of this uncontrollable variety. For individual agencies, the amount of "controllability" ranged from 0 to 100 percent. In the Department of Agriculture, for example, 62 percent of the agency budget is relatively immune to effective budgetary control.[2] For this reason, as well, radical changes are highly unlikely in either the size or the structure of the federal budget.

A third significant characteristic of this budget process concerns the separation of the tax and spending sides of the budget. Because tax measures and appropriation bills are considered by Congress at different times and by different committees (Ways and Means vs. Appropriations), the important proposition that the spending of $1 implies an additional taxes of $1 tends to be forgotten. The implicit failure to weigh the benefits of additional expenditures against the cost of additional taxes has often been cited as a major defect in the budgetary process, at least at the Congressional level.

Finally, the procedures by which the Congress considers appropriation bills, determines budget priorities, and allocates the budget is a most haphazard one. Even the most basic priority and allocation question—that of spending on civilian as opposed to military programs—is not confronted directly in the Congressional appropriation process. Perhaps the best picture of the inadequacy of the appropriation routine was presented in a speech by Repre-

[2] Murray L. Weidenbaum, "Budget 'Uncontrollability' as an Obstacle to Improving the Allocation of Government Resources," in U.S. Congress, Joint Economic Committee, Subcommittee on Economy in Government, *The Analysis and Evaluation of Public Expenditures; The PPB System,* 1969.

sentative Joelson from New Jersey on the floor of the House of Representatives. In his speech, Joelson stated:

Since all appropriation bills have their beginnings in the House, the importance of the House Appropriations Committee is great because it begins the "beginnings." Yet, despite its importance, or perhaps because of it, the Appropriations Committee operates under rules which are as archaic as they are undemocratic . . . . The House Appropriations Committee is composed of 51 members, but is divided into 13 subcommittees, each of which has jurisdiction over a particular prescribed area of governmental activity.

. . . The decisions of the subcommittees are rarely overruled by the full committee, the meetings of which are merely cursory rituals of ratification. Assignment to subcommittees is within the sole discretion of the committee chairman after consultation with the ranking minority members as to minority assignments. In this power of assignment by the chairman is embedded his ability to color all the deliberations of the committee and to shape its decisions in his own image and in conformity with his own political philosophy . . . . Thus, it is understandable that [the current chairman] has constituted himself as chairman of the Defense Subcommittee and has backstopped himself on that subcommittee with members having a similar point of view. For instance, the next ranking member after the chairman is a Congressman who is a major general in the Army Reserves.

On the other hand, if the chairman believes that the funds for a particular program should be curtailed, he need merely assign to the subcommittee in charge a majority of House Members known to be unfriendly to that program. An example is to be found in the composition of the Subcommittee on Labor and Health, Education and Welfare. It is this subcommittee which handles the embattled antipoverty program. . . .

The chairmen of the various subcommittees pretty much run the shows of their panels. They are all very knowledgeable, although not always sympathetic, concerning the agencies and programs under their jurisdiction. They schedule the witnesses . . . . After each witness concludes his statement, it is customary for the subcommittee chairman to question him at length. When he is done not only is the subject usually exhausted, but also so are all participants. If other congressional subcommittee members do any questioning, it usually is very brief.

The subcommittees have great power because the full committee has no way of knowing their recommendations until the very moment of the meeting of the full committee for the purpose of acting upon such recommendations. . . . This system makes full committee meetings perfunctory to the point of being farcical.

Full committee meetings to pass upon the recommendations of subcommittees seldom consume more time than a half hour, although they invariably involve approval of expenditures running into the billions of dollars. . . . The atmosphere hardly lends itself to real deliberation or questioning in depth. A feeling of fantasy assails a person who in a period of time no longer than an hour is expected to vote, for example, on a defense appropriation of $62 billion. Although it may be a heady experience to be spending $1 billion per minute, it is also a most discouraging one.

It should be noted that neither the House nor Senate Appropriations Committees adopt a total budget. Rather, as each subcommittee completes its hearings for the fiscal year, its appropriation bill is brought to the floor. Thus, appropriations are made one at a time and national expenditures grow like Topsy. It is true that each January, the President sends to the Congress a total Federal budget prepared by the Bureau of the Budget, but it is advisory only. The President proposes, but Congress disposes. Furthermore, it disposes on a piecemeal basis which means that never does the Appropriations Committee or the Congress itself decide in advance how percentages or portions of the pie will be divided. A system of priorities is not fixed in advance, and the relative share of each competing claim for Federal money is not known until after the appropriation process is completed.[3]

II. THE STRUCTURE OF THE FEDERAL BUDGET

To examine the structure of the federal budget, both the expenditure and the revenue sides of the account must be analyzed. We shall view the structure of taxes first and then the pattern of expenditures.

A. *Federal Revenue*

On an aggregate level, the structure of federal taxes is a fairly straightforward matter. It is only when one delves beneath the surface of the tax structure that one discovers the "can of worms" which United States tax policy is. We shall delay that below-surface venture until the next chapter. Here we shall discuss the

[3] *Congressional Record,* January 29, 1968, pp. H432-H433.

relative importance of various types of taxes in terms of the total revenue which they provide. We shall also attempt to generalize about who it is that pays federal taxes.

Table 6-1 lists the kinds of federal taxes and the amount of tax

Table 6-1.   U.S. Federal Taxes by Major Source, FY 1969 (Estimated)

| | Revenue | |
| | Amount (Billions of $) | Percentage of Total |
Source		
Personal Income	84.4	45.3
Corporation Income	38.1	20.4
Customs	2.3	1.2
Excise Taxes	14.8	7.9
Motor fuel	4.5	2.4
Alcoholic beverages	4.4[a]	2.3
Tobacco	2.2[a]	1.1
Other	3.7[a]	1.9
Estate and Gift	3.2	1.7
Payroll	40.5	21.7
Other	2.8	1.5
	186.1	100.0

Source. U.S. Treasury Department, *Treasury Bulletin,* pp. 2-3.
[a] Estimated from past trends.

revenue accounted for by each in 1969. As can be seen from the breakdown displayed there, the personal income tax is the major source of revenue to the federal government, providing about 45 percent of the total. This is about twice the revenue provided by either the corporation income tax or payroll taxes—the other two primary revenue earners. It should be noted that most payroll taxes are not available to support general federal expenditures. They go into special funds to cover Social Security benefits and other (mostly transfer) payments. Consequently, the personal income tax and the corporation income tax account for a substantially greater proportion of the monies available to support exhaustive expenditure programs than is indicated by Table 6-1.

Knowing the total amount of revenue raised by federal taxes and the relative importance of each of the taxes, the next logical question is, "Who pays these taxes?" Tables 6-2 and 6-3 provide some evidence on the distribution of the total federal tax bill.

Table 6-2. Percentage Distribution of U.S. Federal Taxes and U.S. Federal Taxes as a Percentage of Income for 1960

Family Income	Individual Income	Corporation Income	Excise	Estate and Gift	Payroll	Total Federal
	Percentage Distribution of Taxes					
0– 2,000	.6	3.4	4.6	—	4.6	2.5
2,000– 3,000	1.7	5.1	7.6	—	8.1	4.4
3,000– 4,000	3.1	5.0	8.8	—	11.0	5.7
4,000– 5,000	4.7	7.4	16.1	—	15.0	8.7
5,000– 7,500	17.4	17.8	38.9	—	34.6	23.3
7,500–10,000	15.2	8.2	11.7	—	14.9	12.8
10,000–or more	57.3	53.1	12.3	100	11.7	42.5
Total	100.0	100.0	100.0	100	100.0	100.0
	Taxes as a Percentage of Income					
0– 2,000	1.8	5.4	4.5	—	6.1	17.8
2,000– 3,000	4.0	6.2	5.7	—	8.2	24.1
3,000– 4,000	6.6	5.4	5.9	—	10.0	27.9
4,000– 5,000	6.7	5.4	7.3	—	9.3	28.7
5,000– 7,500	7.0	3.6	4.9	—	5.9	21.5
7,500–10,000	8.0	2.2	2.0	—	3.4	15.6
10,000–or more	18.0	8.5	1.2	1.4	1.6	30.6

Source. W. Irwin Gillespie, "Effect of Public Expenditures on the Distribution of Income," in R. Musgrave, ed., *Essays in Fiscal Federalism* (Washington: The Brookings Institution, 1965). Reprinted by permission of the publisher.

The top part of Table 6-2 displays the percent of each of the major federal taxes that was paid by people of each income class in 1960. The lower portion of that table shows the proportion of a family's income which is absorbed by these taxes by income class. From this table it is seen that people earning over $10,000 per year pay more than 42 percent of total federal taxes and well over 50 percent of both the personal income and corporation income taxes. However, even though they bear a significant share of the total tax burden, the proportion of their income which they have to pay in federal taxes is smaller than one would expect. While families earning over $10,000 per year paid about 30 percent of their income in taxes, those with low incomes of $2000 to $5000 contributed nearly as large a percentage—about 27.5 percent.

Table 6-3. U.S. Federal Taxes Paid by Residents of Each of 50 States, in Percent of Total, Index of Per Capita Taxes, and Index of Federal Taxes as a Percentage of Income

Region or State	Percent of Total Federal Taxes (1)	Per Capita Taxes Relative to U.S. Average (2)	Taxes as a Percent of Income Relative to U.S. Average (3)
Total, 50 States and District of Columbia	100.00	100.0	100.0
New England	6.73	117.2	107.1
Maine	.43	84.5	101.3
New Hampshire	.36	103.0	109.1
Vermont	.19	92.4	107.1
Massachusetts	3.16	114.7	103.2
Rhode Island	.48	104.5	101.9
Connecticut	2.11	144.0	115.9
Middle Atlantic	22.55	120.1	106.6
New York	12.18	130.8	109.8
New Jersey	4.25	121.0	103.3
Pennsylvania	6.12	103.0	102.8
East North Central	21.50	108.9	100.2
Ohio	5.44	102.9	100.0
Indiana	2.44	96.6	93.5
Illinois	6.81	123.8	103.9
Michigan	4.80	111.4	101.6
Wisconsin	2.01	94.4	94.6
West North Central	7.35	90.1	94.6
Minnesota	1.67	91.6	94.4
Iowa	1.23	87.0	88.2
Missouri	2.35	100.8	105.5
North Dakota	.23	68.0	84.3
South Dakota	.24	67.8	85.5
Nebraska	.66	88.7	93.3
Kansas	.97	83.8	87.0
South Atlantic	13.07	88.0	101.9
Delaware	.50	190.6	158.7
Maryland	2.10	114.7	105.0
District of Columbia	.64	156.4	116.6

Table 6-3. (*Continued*)

Region or State	Percent of Total Federal Taxes (1)	Per Capita Taxes Relative to U.S. Average (2)	Taxes as a Percent of Income Relative to U.S. Average (3)
Virginia	1.99	87.0	98.8
West Virginia	.65	70.3	95.6
North Carolina	1.77	69.8	92.4
South Carolina	.78	59.0	86.7
Georgia	1.68	74.3	93.7
Florida	2.95	98.4	111.3
East South Central	4.18	63.4	89.9
Kentucky	1.10	67.4	89.9
Tennessee	1.41	71.3	95.6
Alabama	1.10	61.5	88.3
Mississippi	.57	48.0	80.9
West South Central	7.30	76.2	93.3
Arkansas	.58	57.7	85.7
Louisiana	1.23	66.9	87.5
Oklahoma	.99	77.8	93.7
Texas	4.50	82.4	96.1
Mountain	3.46	87.4	96.5
Montana	.30	83.5	94.9
Idaho	.27	75.5	89.4
Wyoming	.16	97.4	104.6
Colorado	.95	95.1	96.6
New Mexico	.38	74.0	91.8
Arizona	.70	85.9	99.6
Utah	.41	79.3	93.1
Nevada	.28	127.1	106.3
Pacific	13.86	110.0	96.0
Washington	1.51	97.7	91.3
Oregon	.97	96.8	97.6
California	10.92	114.4	97.1
Alaska	.13	93.3	80.1
Hawaii	.33	90.1	87.1

Source. U.S. Congress, Committee on Government Operations, "Federal Revenue and Expenditure Estimates for States and Regions, Fiscal Years 1965–67," Washington, 1968.

The numbers in the lower half of Table 6-2 make it possible to discover whether any particular tax is progressive or regressive. If the proportion of income absorbed by taxes goes up as the level of income rises, our definition from Chapter 5 tells us that the tax is progressive. If the proportion goes down as income rises, the tax is regressive. On this basis, the personal income tax is seen to be a progressive tax, the percentage rising from 1.8 to 18.0. On the other hand, excise and payroll taxes are progressive up to about $4000 or $5000, after which they turn seriously regressive. The last column of the table shows that the entire tax structure tends to balance the varied incidence patterns of the individual taxes. The total tax structure appears to be slightly progressive, except for the regressive segment from $5000 to $10,000. The dip in the tax rate through this income range, it should be noted, is due to the rather strange incidence pattern of the corporation income tax.

Table 6-3 presents some additional evidence on who pays the taxes. In that table, the percentage of total federal taxes paid by the residents of each of the 50 states is shown. The table also displays an index of the amount of taxes paid per person in each of the states and an index of the percent of the income of the people in the state which goes for federal taxes.[4] Not surprisingly, the states of New York and California supply the largest amounts of tax revenue to the federal government. They are both large and rich. Taken together, residents of these two states account for nearly one-fourth of the total federal tax bill. The very small states of Alaska and Wyoming are found at the other end of the scale. Together, these states contribute less than one-fourth of one percent of total Federal taxes.

In terms of per capita taxes, Delaware ranks the highest. There the average citizen pays nearly twice as much in taxes to the federal government each year as does the average United States citizen.[5] Mississippi and Arkansas rank the lowest, paying about

[4] The figures in both columns 2 and 3 are indexes. In both columns, the figure for the entire United States is taken to be 100 and the figure of each state and region is stated relative to 100. Thus, if a state displays a figure of 110 in column 2, it means that its per capita taxes are 110 percent of those of the Nation as a whole.

[5] In the last few years, about $600 to $700 of federal taxes are paid by each

one-half as much per person as the national average. This is a result of the significantly lower per capita incomes in these states.[6]

As can be seen by the last column of Table 6-3, the range of federal taxes as a percentage of income among the states extends from 80 percent of the national average to about 160 percent. Again, Delaware ranks first. The percent of its income paid in federal taxes is nearly 160 percent of the United States average. Alaska and Mississippi rank last with a ratio only slightly above 80 percent.

B. *Federal Expenditures*

Just as the structure of federal revenue has several dimensions, so too does the structure of federal spending. Two relevant dimensions are implied by these questions: "Who does the spending?" "For what programs are expenditures made?" The budget document presented by the President to Congress contains evidence on both of these questions. There expenditures are presented both by the agency which does the spending and by the function or type of program to which the expenditure will be applied. Tables 6-4 and 6-5 summarize these two breakdowns for the President's Fiscal Year 1969 budget.

In Table 6-4, the total budget is presented according to the function or activity for which expenditures are made. The level of military expenditures was expected to be about $52 billion in FY 1969—the largest function in the budget. It should be noted that this $52.0 billion does not include another $29.2 billion of military expenditures for the Vietnam War.[7] The other major item in the budget is that for the social expenditures of health, labor, and welfare. Included in this figure are the benefit payments in

United States citizen. This figures out to approximately 20 percent of the average person's income.

[6] It should be noted that the numbers in Table 6-3 are, in some cases, very rough estimates. This is so because of the difficulty in tracing the incidence of those taxes which can be shifted, such as the corporation income tax. For example, it is generally agreed that Delaware ranks higher in this table than it should because it is the home of many of the nation's largest corporations. In allocating the corporation income tax, the location of the firm's main office was given more weight than it properly deserves.

[7] Many have argued that this number underestimates total FY 1969 government expenditures on Vietnam.

Table 6-4.   Federal Budget Outlays, FY 1969, by Function[a]

Function	Outlays (Billions of $)	Percent
National defense (except Vietnam)	52.2	27.6
International affairs (except Vietnam)	3.9	2.0
Vietnam	29.2	15.5
Space research and technology	4.2	2.2
Agriculture and agric. resources	5.4	2.9
Natural resources	1.9	1.0
Commerce and transportation	8.0	4.2
Housing and community development	2.3	1.2
Health and welfare	48.8	25.8
Education and manpower	7.1	3.8
Veterans benefits and services	7.7	4.1
Interest on public debt	15.2	8.0
Other	3.0	1.6
Total	188.9	100.0

Source. The Budget of the United States Government, 1970, p. 69.
[a] Excluding intragovernmental transactions.

the Social Security and Medicare programs. Between them, these expenditures account for nearly three-fourths of the federal budget. Similar patterns are observed when the budget is organized along agency lines in Table 6-5.

Tables 6-6 and 6-7 show how federal expenditures are allocated among people of different income levels and status. These data are analogous to those of Tables 6-2 and 6-3 which showed the distribution of the tax burden. The data in these tables answer the question: "On behalf of whom are federal expenditures undertaken?"

Table 6-6 presents the allocation of 1960 federal expenditures among families of various income classes. Because of their size, the Social Security and general expenditures categories account for most of the income distributional impact of federal expenditures. As seen from the table, Social Security expenditures form a significant proportion of the income of poorer families. It is primarily for this reason that the lower and lower-middle income classes show as high a percentage of public spending receipts rela-

Table 6-5. Federal Budget Outlays, FY 1969, by Agency[a]

Agency	Outlays (Billions of $)	Percent
Legislative and Judiciary	.4	.2
The President's Office	5.2	2.8
Department of Agriculture	7.7	4.1
Department of Commerce	.9	.5
Department of Defense	79.0	41.8
Department of Health, Education, and Welfare	46.3	24.5
Department of Housing and Urban Development	2.0	1.1
Department of the Interior	.5	.3
Department of Justice	.5	.3
Department of Labor	3.7	2.0
Post Office	.9	.5
Department of State	.4	.2
Department of Transportation	6.0	3.2
Treasury Department	16.3	8.6
Atomic Energy Commission	2.5	1.3
National Aeronautics and Space Administration	4.2	2.2
Veterans Administration	7.7	4.0
Other	4.7	2.5
Total	188.9	100.0

Source. *The Budget of the United States Government*, 1970, p. 487.
[a] Excluding intragovernmental transactions.

tive to income as implied in the final column of Table 6-6. Indeed, for families in the very lowest income category, the "benefits" from federal expenditures equal about 85 percent of family income.

An important point should be made with respect to these numbers—especially those in the general expenditures category. The distributions shown in Table 6-6 are based on reasonable assumptions about who gains from the various forms of public spending. However, for expenditures on public goods (for example, national defense), it is difficult, if not impossible, to assign the benefits precisely to different people. The data shown in the general expenditures column assume that the benefits from these public goods are distributed among the people as the nation's income, in general, is distributed. Because these general expenditures are

Table 6-6. U.S. Federal Expenditures as a Percentage of Income, 1960

Family Income	Housing	Education	Social Security and Veterans	Agriculture	Health	General Expenditures[a]	Interest	Total
$0– 2,000	.4	.1	66.0	1.7	.9	14.5	1.8	85.4
2,000– 3,000	.3	.2	18.6	1.4	.4	14.3	1.5	36.7
3,000– 4,000	.2	.2	13.4	.9	.3	14.8	1.3	31.1
4,000– 5,000	.1	.1	6.0	.3	.2	15.3	.8	22.8
5,000– 7,500	—	.1	2.7	.2	.1	13.9	.5	17.5
7,500–10,000	.0	.1	1.5	.3	.1	12.6	.6	15.2
10,000–or more	.0	.1	.5	.3	.1	13.5	1.7	16.2

Source. See Table 6-2.
[a] General Expenditures include those for national defense, international affairs, and miscellaneous.

about one-half of total federal spending, different, yet reasonable, assumptions could substantially change the pattern shown in the final column.

In Table 6-7 the geographic location of the recipients of federal government expenditures is shown. This table is the analogue of Table 6-3.[8] Although, as we have seen, New York and California supply the largest volume of tax revenue to the federal government, they also receive the largest amounts of federal expenditures. Taken together, these two states are on the receiving end of about 20 percent of total federal government spending. In per capita terms, however, New York receives only about 82 percent of the average national per capita expenditure, while California receives about one and one-half times the national per capita expenditure. In terms of per capita expenditures received (relative to the U.S. average), Alaska, Hawaii, and the District of Columbia rank at the top with over 200 percent of the national average in each case; Michigan and Wisconsin rank at the bottom, each receiving less than two-thirds of the national per capita expenditure.

The final column of Table 6-7 compares each state in terms of federal expenditures received as a percent of income. Two factors explain a state's relative position in this calculation—how much federal spending it receives and the size of the total income. The more spending the state receives, the higher its rank. Conversely, the richer a state, the lower its rank. The states at the top of this list are again Alaska, Hawaii, and the District of Columbia. In this calculation, the southern and Mountain states tend to rank

[8] Again, the numbers in this table are open to question. Many public expenditures are as difficult to trace regionally as, for example, corporation income tax revenues. Estimates for the distribution of many of the expenditures are based on nothing more than reasonable assumptions. For other expenditures, not even this can be claimed. For example, defense contracts are allocated to the state of the prime contractor even though he may subcontract out much of the contract to firms in other states. Even if there were no subcontracting, this estimating procedure would be open to question. There is no reason to believe that the regional distribution of the benefits of national defense is anything like the distribution of defense contracts. For an excellent discussion of the difficulty of allocating both revenues and expenditures among states, see Selma Mushkin, "Federal Grants and Federal Expenditures," *National Tax Journal*, X (3), September 1957, pp. 193-213.

Table 6-7. U.S. Federal Expenditures Allocated to Residents of Each of 50 States, in Percent of Total, Index of Per Capita Expenditures, and Index of Expenditures as a Percentage of Income

Region or State	Percent of Total Federal Expenditures	Per Capita Expenditures Received Relative to U.S. Average	Expenditures as a Percent of Income Relative to U.S. Average
Total, 50 States and District of Columbia	100.00	100.0	100.0
New England	6.36	110.8	101.2
Maine	.49	98.1	117.6
New Hampshire	.30	86.6	91.7
Vermont	.21	98.5	114.2
Massachusetts	2.85	103.6	93.2
Rhode Island	.56	122.2	119.2
Connecticut	1.95	132.7	106.7
Middle Atlantic	14.99	79.8	70.8
New York	7.60	81.6	68.5
New Jersey	3.03	86.2	73.6
Pennsylvania	4.36	73.3	73.2
East North Central	13.80	69.9	64.3
Ohio	3.82	72.2	70.2
Indiana	1.84	72.7	70.4
Illinois	4.04	73.4	61.6
Michigan	2.76	64.1	58.4
Wisconsin	1.35	63.2	63.4
West North Central	8.44	103.4	108.7
Minnesota	1.56	85.2	87.8
Iowa	1.23	87.1	88.3
Missouri	2.56	110.1	115.1
North Dakota	.47	141.7	175.7
South Dakota	.40	112.6	142.1
Nebraska	.83	110.9	116.7
Kansas	1.40	120.3	124.9
South Atlantic	17.88	120.5	139.4
Delaware	.27	102.1	84.9
Maryland	2.82	153.9	140.9
District of Columbia	1.33	334.6	249.5
Virginia	3.44	150.4	170.8

Table 6-7. (*Continued*)

Region or State	Percent of Total Federal Expenditures	Per Capita Expenditures Received Relative to U.S. Average	Expenditures as a Percent of Income Relative to U.S. Average
West Virginia	.66	71.1	96.6
North Carolina	2.14	34.4	111.8
South Carolina	1.23	93.6	137.5
Georgia	2.46	113.1	142.6
Florida	3.38	112.7	127.4
East South Central	5.65	85.6	121.4
Kentucky	1.45	88.7	118.4
Tennessee	1.58	79.7	106.9
Alabama	1.67	92.9	133.5
Mississippi	.96	80.2	135.2
West South Central	9.81	92.5	125.5
Arkansas	.75	75.1	111.4
Louisiana	1.63	83.5	115.7
Oklahoma	1.35	106.5	128.2
Texas	6.03	111.3	129.8
Mountain	4.62	116.9	129.0
Montana	.46	127.7	145.2
Idaho	.35	87.7	103.9
Wyoming	.24	148.7	153.4
Colorado	1.26	125.9	127.8
New Mexico	.64	124.6	154.5
Arizona	93	113.7	131.8
Utah	54	104.0	122.1
Nevada	.24	110.1	92.1
Pacific	18.44	146.3	127.8
Washington	1.87	120.4	112.6
Oregon	.78	78.4	79.1
California	14.45	151.4	128.5
Alaska	.50	435.4	373.6
Hawaii	.75	201.3	194.6

Source. See Table 6-3.

high; federal expenditures received by nearly all of them are a greater proportion of their income than the national average. At the bottom of the list are Michigan and Illinois, which show expenditures received relative to income of only 60 percent of the national average. In general, the northern industrial states receive a substantially lower level of federal expenditures relative to income than does the rest of the nation.

From the first and second columns of Tables 6-3 and 6-7, the *net effect* of federal taxes and spending in any given state can be calculated. Because the numbers in these columns can be directly transformed into dollars, statements of the following sort can be made. For every $12.18 that New York contributes in federal taxes, it gets $7.60 back in expenditures; for every $10.92 that California contributes in taxes, it gets $14.45 back in expenditures; for every $124 paid in taxes by an Illinois *resident,* $73 is received in expenpenditures; for every $74 paid in taxes by a Georgia *resident,* $113 is received in expenditures.[9] This comparison shows that the New England and East North Central states tend to pay more in federal revenues than they receive in expenditures. The reverse holds for all of the other regions of the country.

Similar to the *geographic* redistribution of income caused by the federal tax and expenditure system is its effect on the redistribution of income among people of different income levels. How much do poor people pay in taxes relative to the amount they receive in federal expenditures? How about rich people? While some evidence on this matter was presented in Tables 6-2 and 6-6, the results of a more detailed study were summarized in a recent article.

Between the progressive income tax and the total fiscal operations of government (how much government gets, from where, and on what it spends its revenue), the redistribution of income in favor of low-income groups . . . is taking place in a very substantial way. In 1965, the most recent year for which such figures are available, it has been authoritatively estimated that those with incomes under $2,000 got back $3.88 in benefits for every dollar of tax they paid. In fact, benefits received exceeded taxes paid up to the $5,999 income class, at

[9] The first two of these assertions are made by comparing numbers in the first column of Tables 6-3 and 6-7. The second two statements rely on numbers in the second column of these tables.

which point taxes and benefits canceled each other out. In the $6,000–$7,499 income class, benefits received were worth only 89 cents for every dollar of taxes paid; in the $7,500–$9,999 class, benefits received fell to 78 cents [for every dollar of taxes paid], then to 65 cents for the $10,000-$14,499 income class; and finally, to 37 cents for those in the $15,000-and-more income group.[10]

III. SUMMARY AND CONCLUSIONS

In this chapter, the "facts" of the federal budget were discussed. This overview is a prelude to the next two chapters which focus on the revenue and the expenditure sides of the budget account, respectively. In the first part of the chapter, the long and arduous route followed by the budget during the year and a half in which it is constructed, debated, and passed was outlined. This prolonged and complex procedure was viewed as both necessary for the effective operation of "checks and balances" and seriously afflicted by an institutional arrangement guaranteeing haphazard Congressional consideration of the budget. Both the construction and the structure of the budget were seen as precluding rapid shifts in spending patterns and budget allocations.

In the second part of the chapter, the pattern and sources of federal revenues and expenditures were examined. Attempts were made to answer the twin questions: "Who pays the taxes?" "Who gets the benefits of the expenditures?" As was noted, the answers to these questions are neither simple nor straightforward. Some federal taxes are regressive and others are progressive. Overall the federal tax structure is progressive through some income ranges and regressive through others. Much the same can be said about federal expenditures. However, it is undeniable that the federal revenue and expenditure system redistributes, both among income classes and geographically, an enormous amount of the nation's income.

[10] Haig Babian, "Can Taxes Do More than Raise Revenue?" *Saturday Review*, March 22, 1969, p. 32.

7

The Federal Tax System—Its Impact on Efficiency, Equity, and Stability

In this chapter, we leave the vantage point of overview and generalization and delve into the details—the nitty-gritty—of the federal tax system. We have seen that the lion's share of federal government revenue is accounted for by four basic taxes. These are the personal income tax, the corporate income tax, payroll taxes, and excise taxes. If "earmarked" taxes—those which are paid directly into special funds—are deducted from the total tax revenue, personal and corporate income taxes account for about 80 percent of the "General Fund" revenue of the government. In this chapter, we shall concentrate on these two kinds of taxes.

In Chapter 5, we argued that the imposition of taxes affects the economy by altering both the allocation of resources (economic efficiency) and the distribution of income (equity). There is yet a third criterion by which the "worth" of a tax is often judged. This is the contribution of the tax to (or its detraction from) *economic stability*. If a tax automatically tends to stimulate an economy when it is entering a recession or to restrain spending in an economy which is inflationary, it has a stabilizing influence on the economy. If its impacts are in the opposite direction, it is said to be destabilizing. Because economic stability is a basic social goal, we shall consider this criterion as well.[1]

[1] There is a fourth important criterion in evaluating a tax which should also be mentioned. This is the difficulty of administering the tax which gets re-

I. THE FEDERAL PERSONAL INCOME TAX

The personal income tax is a tax levied by the federal government on the incomes of private individuals. It is, therefore, a direct tax —its incidence falls on the individual who is taxed; in general, its burden cannot be shifted. As a direct tax on income, the effect of the personal income tax on the relative prices of goods and services is likely to be small, especially as compared with an excise or consumption tax. The resource allocation or efficiency impact of the tax, therefore, must occur through its effect on incentives and capacities to work and to invest—D_e, D_i, A_e, and A_i. Because it is a tax on people's earnings, the income tax will have an equity impact through its direct alteration of the distribution of income.

The personal income tax, contrary to common belief, is not levied on all of the kinds of personal income which people receive. The basic income concept in the tax structure is the concept of *adjusted gross income*. Some kinds of income, called *exclusions*, are omitted from the calculation of this figure. The items excluded from gross income (in obtaining adjusted gross income) include social security and unemployment compensation benefits received by people, the interest received on state and local government bonds, and many kinds of fringe benefits which are furnished to employees by employers. Because the amount of tax paid depends on what gets included in adjusted gross income, these kinds of excluded income are "tax free."[2]

flected in the total dead-weight cost of tax collection and enforcement. G.L.S. Shackle stated this consideration well:

Since any work or trouble that the actual collection of taxes entails does no good to anybody, and is pure loss, it is plain that if two systems are in other respects equal, that one will be better which leaves the smaller gap between the yearly total collected from the taxpayers and the portion of this which remains available for the government to spend after it has paid the tax collectors for their work. (*Economics for Pleasure* (London: Cambridge University Press, 2nd Edition, 1968), p. 221.)

Moreover, in addition to the costs of collection and enforcement, there are also the deadweight costs of compliance with the tax code. For many taxes, the time and knowledge required for calculating the tax and filling out the tax forms are enormous. These compliance costs, it should be noted, are borne by taxpayers in the private sector.

[2] It should be noted that adjusted gross income is a "money-payment"

While adjusted gross income is a basic income tax notion, a number of things are subtracted from this concept before the value is obtained to which tax rates are applied. These items to be deducted from adjusted gross income are called *deductions*.[3] The value that is obtained after deductions are subtracted from adjusted gross income is called *taxable income*. Included among deductions are contributions to charities, interest that is paid (on, say, personal loans), other taxes such as sales taxes, and a certain amount of doctor, hospital, drug, and dentist bills.[4] In addition to these deductions, which take the form of expenses or contributions, the tax law permits an additional flat deduction (called an *exemption*) of $600 for the taxpayer plus an additional $600 for each of the people whom he supports (called *dependents*).[5] Moreover, additional exemptions can be claimed if the taxpayer or his spouse is blind or is over 64 years of age. It is after subtracting all of these deductions and exemptions that the taxable income figure is obtained. It is to this number that tax rates are applied in computing the tax bill.

In computing the amount of taxes which must be paid, the taxpayer consults a tax schedule. The schedule applicable for 1970[6] is shown in Table 7-1 for a married couple filing their tax return

notion. That is, only money payments are considered to be income. This differs from the economist's definition of income which envisions a flow of goods and services over a period of time. To the economist, the food grown on a farm and consumed by the farmer or the value of services of the house lived in by the home owner are part of an individual's *real income*. Because they are not money payments, however, they are not included in the tax collector's definition of adjusted gross income.

[3] The difference between exclusions and deductions, then, is that exclusions never get counted in adjusted gross income, while deductions get subtracted from adjusted gross income after it is calculated.

[4] The income tax law does not require taxpayers to list in detail these deductions if they prefer not to. In lieu of itemizing deductions, the taxpayer can use a standard deduction. In 1969, the standard deduction had a maximum of 10 percent of adjusted gross income up to $1000 per married couple. Recent legislation has increased these amounts beginning in 1971.

[5] The tax reform legislation of 1969 scheduled a series of increases in the personal exemption, up to $750 by 1973.

[6] It should be noted that this schedule does not take account of the surtax provision which is presumably a temporary feature of the U.S. personal income tax structure. This surtax simply adds a fixed percentage (originally 10 percent) to the taxpayer's tax bill.

Table 7-1.   Federal Income Tax Rates, Joint Returns, 1968

Taxable Income (Dollars)	Tax Rates (Percentages)
0– 1,000	14
1,000– 2,000	15
2,000– 3,000	16
3,000– 4,000	17
4,000– 8,000	19
8,000– 12,000	22
12,000– 16,000	25
16,000– 20,000	28
20,000– 40,000	32–45
40,000–100,000	48–60
100,000–200,000	62–69
over 200,000	70

Source. Internal Revenue Code.

jointly.[7] This table is read as follows: 14 percent of the first $1000 of taxable income must be paid in taxes; 15 percent of the taxable income from $1000 to $2000 must be paid in taxes; and so on, up to a tax rate of 70 percent which is paid on all taxable income above $200,000. Thus, the tax rate on *additional* units of taxable income rises as the level of income rises. These tax rates are *marginal tax rates* because they apply to the additional or marginal dollars of income. Since the marginal rate of taxes rises as income rises, it is above the average tax rate and, hence, it pulls the average up with it.[8] Consequently, in this tax structure, the proportion of a person's taxable income paid in taxes (the average tax rate) rises as his taxable income rises. According to our previous definition, this signifies that the personal income tax is a progressive tax.[9]

[7] The tax law permits married couples to file a single joint return even though only one person has an income. In a joint return, the total income of the couple is split equally between the two. Because the income tax is a progressive tax, this has real tax saving advantages to the married couple who files jointly. This saving is discussed later.

[8] This, it will be recalled, is a basic relationship of marginal analysis. "If the marginal is above the average, the average will rise; if the marginal is below the average, the average will fall."

[9] We shall see later that this conclusion may be modified because of some special provisions in the tax law.

To understand the income tax structure more clearly, let us work through a simple tax calculation. This example incorporates the basic notions of adjustable gross income, taxable income, exemptions, exclusions, and deductions. Assume a family with three children, in which the husband earned $8000 in a year and the wife earned $1800 for part-time work. In addition, assume that the family received $200 in interest on some state bonds that it owns and $500 in dividends on stock. They gave away $350 to charity, paid $750 in interest on their home mortgage, were charged $400 in sales and other taxes, and spent $800 for college tuition. In Table 7-2, their income tax is calculated. In working

Table 7-2.   Hypothetical Income Tax Calculation For a Family with Three Children

Adjusted Gross Income[a]—$8000 + $1800 + $500	= $10,300
Less deductions[b]—($350 + $750 + $400) = $1500	− 1,500
	8,800
Less *exemptions*—(5 × $600) = $3000	− 3,000
equals *taxable income*	$ 5,800
Tax on first $1000 of taxable income = $140	
Tax on taxable income from $1000–$2000 = 150	
Tax on taxable income from $2000–$3000 = 160	
Tax on taxable income from $3000–$4000 = 170	
Tax on taxable income from $4000–$5000 = 190	
Tax on taxable income from $5000–$5800 = 152	
Total tax $962	

[a] The interest on state bonds is not included. It is an exclusion and is not added into adjusted gross income.
[b] The college tuition is not an allowable deduction.

through this calculation, it should be noted that each step follows directly from the basic definitions and structure of the tax, as we have outlined them.[10]

A. *Special Provisions*

Built into the personal income tax structure are a large number of special provisions, each of which gives preferred treatment to

[10] It is interesting to note how the increased personal exemption written into the tax reform legislation of 1969 decreases taxable income and tax liability. An interesting exercise is to recalculate the taxes owed by this hypothetical family under the $750 personal exemption scheduled to go into effect in 1973.

certain people or certain activities. Because these special provisions benefit certain classes of people and affect particular kinds of economic activities, questions of both "fairness" and efficiency are pertinent in judging each case. The question which must be answered in judging social policy by the standard of the Principle of Maximum Social Gain is: "Does the net effect of the redistribution of income and the reallocation of resources implicit in each of these special provisions add to the welfare of the people? Is the social value of the net gains to those who are favored greater than the social value of the net income reductions to those who are hurt?" Clearly, an individual's value judgments will affect how he answers these questions in any given case. As a number of these special provisions are discussed, each reader should attempt to apply his own judgments on the social welfare gains and losses of the income redistributions that are implied.[11]

1. *Tax Exempt Securities.* According to the tax law, people who own state and local government bonds do not have to pay income tax on the interest which they receive from holding these bonds. Because of this provision, many very rich people place their wealth in these kinds of securities. It provides them with a tax shelter, a means for effectively reducing the income tax rate that applies to them. For example, by switching their assets from, say, corporation to municipal bonds, individuals in the highest tax bracket can reduce the tax rate on interest income from 70 percent to 0 percent. Because of this exclusion, taxpayers holding no state or local bonds must pay higher taxes if the income tax structure is to yield a given amount of tax revenue.[12]

In addition to the tax break given these bond holders, there are

---

[11] In our brief discussion of these special provisions we shall emphasize their equity impact rather than their very real effect on the allocation of resources.

[12] With respect to this special provision, former Senator Paul Douglas noted:

When Mrs. Horace Dodge, Sr., inherited $56 million for the estate of her husband, she immediately invested all of it in state and municipal bonds and thereby removed the entire income from her fortune from federal taxation. This is a particularly attractive tax route for those in the upper income tax brackets who do not wish to play an active role in the business world. If only the existing income from these bond issues were taxed, federal receipts would be at least 50 percent on the $3½ billion that is now immune from federal taxation. This would amount to $1¾ billion.

(*continued on p. 118*)

some additional effects of this provision which should be noted. For one thing, cities and states can borrow more easily than they could otherwise because of this provision, and at a lower rate.[13] Consequently, cities and states have been able to float bonds for the construction of schools, roads, and other public facilities more cheaply and easily than otherwise. Presumably, more of these facilities have been constructed because of this provision than would have had it not existed. People who make use of these public facilities, therefore, stand to gain by this special provision of the tax law.

In recent years, the amount of borrowing undertaken by cities and states has risen rapidly. As the supply of bonds has increased, the price has consequently tended to fall and the interest rate on state and local bonds has tended to rise (though it is still below that of corporation bonds). Because of the growth in total state and local borrowing together with the higher interest rate, the interest earned by the holders of these tax-free bonds has risen. Consequently, this tax loophole has become increasingly important. As would be expected from these effects, the political forces opposing the abolition of this special provision are the wealthy and the state and local governments.[14]

2. *Capital Gains.* The forms in which people receive income are many—wages, profits, rental income, interest, royalties for writing books, and so on. A proper definition of "income" for tax purposes would include payments from all of these different sources. In point of fact, it does not. In addition to interest from state and local government bonds, there is another form of income which comes in for special treatment in the personal in-

"The Problem of Tax Loopholes," *American Scholar*, Winter, 1967-68, p. 34.

[13] Because of the favorable tax status of these securities, the demand for them has been higher than it would have been otherwise, implying a somewhat lower interest rate. It should be noted that people holding these bonds, while gaining tax exemption, receive this lower interest rate.

[14] It has been estimated that cities and states currently save about $1.25 billion each year because of the lower interest rate which they have to pay. On the other hand, the Federal Government loses about $1.75 billion each year because of the tax-exempt status of the bonds. Thus, the Federal Government would save about $.5 billion each year if it just directly subsidized cities by the amount which they gain from the tax-free bond provision.

come tax law. This is the income that is received by people when something that they own increases in value. For example, if a person bought a building for $20,000 and sold it the next year for $25,000, having only done ordinary upkeep on it, he would, in effect, have received $5000 of income. This increment in the value of assets is called *capital gains income*.[15] The same kind of capital gain occurs if I sell my 15 shares of Freuhauf Trailer Corporation stock after its price has risen.

The income tax law separates out capital gains income from other forms and subjects it to preferential treatment. The basic provision in the tax law states that the tax rate on capital gains income is *one-half* of the tax rate on other kinds of income—and then only a maximum rate of 25 percent.[16] Consequently, all people, but especially rich people, gain if they can arrange to receive their income in the form of capital gains. For a person in the top tax bracket, it means the difference between paying 70¢ of each additional dollar in taxes and paying only 25¢.

Because of this provision, people have spent a great deal of time and energy searching for ways to switch other kinds of income into capital gains income. For example, corporation stockholders would prefer to see their corporation retain profits in the business (causing expansion and an increase in the value of the stock) rather than pay them to owners (stockholders) in the form of dividends. The regular income tax rates of Table 7-1 apply to income from dividends, but the much lower rate applies to capital gains income. The effect of this has been two-fold: first, corporations now tend to finance their expansion "internally" through retaining profits. Therefore, they bypass the capital market, which is the "economic" way for savings to get fed back into investment. Second, people who own corporation stock pay less in taxes than they otherwise would; other people must then pay higher taxes.

Another example of how noncapital gains income can be trans-

---

[15] According to the tax law, the $5,000 becomes capital gain only after the property is held for six months, sold, and the income realized. If the person dies before he realizes his capital gains income, the law assumes that there has been no capital gain at all.

[16] The tax reform legislation of 1969, it should be noted, placed a limit of $50,000 on the amount of an individual's annual capital gains income which is eligible for the preferential 25 percent tax rate.

formed into capital gains is the now prominent device of the "stock option." Instead of paying executives higher salaries subject to regular income taxation, some companies now give them the option to buy corporation stock at a lower-than-market price. By exercising the option, and then, after a time, selling the stock on the market, the executive receives capital gains income which is taxed at low rates instead of a higher salary which is taxed at normal rates. The corporation gains, the executive gains, and the rest of the taxpayers lose.[17]

In addition to generating artificial techniques for changing the form of income, the existence of the capital gains provision has diverted substantial energy from activities that produce normally taxed income to activities that result in capital gains returns. In some cases this diversion results in lower productivity for the nation. This is so because many activities which generate capital gains income are speculative in nature and do not add to the nation's real output. On the other hand, because some capital gains are generated by productive investments in capital facilities, the preferential treatment may in some cases have the effect of stimulating investment and increasing the nation's output.

3. *Home Owners, the Married, and the Aged.* The income tax law gives preferred treatment to people who own homes relative to those who rent, to the married relative to bachelors, and to the old relative to the young. It would be stretching the case only a little to say that the tax law rewards people for getting married, for buying a house, and for growing old.

The law benefits married people through the "income-splitting" provision. This provision permits a married couple to total their separate incomes, divide the total in one-half (hence, the term "splitting"), and then calculate the tax as if there were two incomes each equal to one-half of the total. Because the tax structure is progressive, the income-splitting provision allows those who can take advantage of it to reduce the amount of tax which

[17] In the words of former Senator Douglas, "'It [the stock option] was touted as a means of helping young executives to climb the economic ladder more rapidly, although in practice the major rewards went to those in the later afternoon of their business careers. Often as members of the boards of directors, they voted themselves these large tax-free bonuses." Paul Douglas, *op. cit.*, p. 33.

they have to pay. In effect, the high tax portion of the larger income gets chopped off and added to the smaller income where it is subject to a lower tax rate.[18]

The tax system benefits homeowners relative to those who rent because of the interest and state and local tax *deduction*[19] provisions. When a person places his financial assets in stocks, bonds, or real investment and receives the income generated by that investment, he pays tax on this income. A person who places his assets in a home is investing just like the person who buys bonds. Instead of receiving interest, the homeowner receives the use of the home as his return. He does not, however, have to pay income tax on this "rental value" return. Because this return is *not* included in his adjusted gross income, it would make sense that he *not* be allowed to count (and deduct from income) expenses connected with the home, such as property taxes. He is allowed to deduct these, however. On the other hand, people who rent are not allowed to deduct rental payments from their income before calculating their taxes.

People who are over 65 and those who are blind receive preferential treatment by being permitted to exempt an additional $600 from their income for tax purposes. In addition, the aged pay no tax on their social security income and some other pensions and get to deduct all of their medical expenses. To question these special provisions is, in some eyes, like hating children and being unpatriotic. It should be noted, however, that people other than the aged and the blind are in adverse circumstances, but they are not given special allowance in the tax system. One has only to think of the crippled, the poorly educated, those with low intelligence, and those subject to social and economic discrimination. Perhaps all special circumstances cannot be ameliorated by means of preferential provisions in the income tax structure! In any case, it

[18] For example, assume a man with $10,000 taxable income and a woman with no taxable income. If they are not married, the man pays taxes of $2190 according to the rate structure of Table 7-1 (and assuming a $600 personal exemption). If they are married, the income could be split between the two people, and the tax calculated as if each person earned half. The total tax in this case would be $1820—a saving of $370 for getting married.
[19] It should be noted that this refers to the deduction for state and local taxes paid and not to the tax-exempt interest received on state and local government bonds.

is the criterion implied by the Principle of Maximum Social Gain which must be applied to these provisions as well as to the others.

The effect of all of these special provisions in the tax law is to seriously erode the amount of total income which is subject to income taxes. Because of all of the exemptions, deductions, and other special provisions, only slightly more than one-half of the nation's personal income is included in taxable income and, hence, subject to taxes. This "erosion" of the tax base must result in higher tax rates if the tax structure is to generate a given level of revenue.

B. *Efficiency and Equity*

Our discussion of the structure of the personal income tax has touched on a number of *equity* considerations. First, as a progressive tax, it is clearly in accord with what has traditionally been known as the "ability to pay" principle. The structure of the tax also reflects the judgment that a dollar taken away from a rich man reduces the society's welfare by less than a dollar taken away from a poor man. Finally, while it does reduce the disparity in people's incomes, the personal income tax is a substantially weaker instrument for equalizing incomes than it is generally believed to be. This is because of the large number of special provisions which can be used to reduce the taxes paid on certain types of income—especially the kinds of income which those in higher income classes tend to receive.

In addition to its equity impacts, the income tax also has *efficiency* effects—because of the tax, resources get allocated differently than they would otherwise be. Because it is a direct tax on income, it alters the willingness and the ability of people to work and invest rather than directly modifying the structure of relative prices. A number of observations can be made. First, it has been argued that the income tax is a *disincentive to saving* (and, therefore, to investment) relative to consumption. It is suggested that not only is the income which is saved taxed but also the earnings generated by the invested savings are taxed—a double taxation argument. However, few now believe that returns from an income generating investment asset should not be subject to taxation. The income generated by capital is not, in substance, different than the income generated by labor.

Second, the income tax may affect people's *willingness to work*. As we have seen, there is reason to believe that the progressivity of the tax reduces the incentive to work. On the other hand, the tax may cause people to work harder than they otherwise would. The first of these effects may result from the effect of the tax in reducing the monetary reward attributable to effort. The second effect may occur if people increase their work effort in order to maintain a given level of living. Joseph Pechman has summarized the existing evidence on this matter as follows.

The evidence suggests that income taxation does not reduce the amount of labor supplied by workers and managers. Work habits are not easily changed and there is little scope in modern industrial society for most people to vary hours of work or the intensity of their efforts in response to changes in tax rates. Nearly all people who are asked about income taxation grumble about it, but relatively few state that they work fewer hours or exert less than their best efforts to avoid being taxed.[20]

Third, the influence of the tax on the *willingness to invest* is complicated by the capital gains provision of the income tax. It is generally believed that the preferential treatment of capital gains largely eliminates whatever adverse effects the basic income tax structure might have on the willingness to invest. Moreover, the tax law permits an investor whose investment loses money to spread out the loss over a large number of years. Because of this procedure, the losing investor's taxes are reduced in each of these years. The effect of this is to reduce the risk involved in investing —again reducing whatever adverse effects on the willingness to invest may be caused by the income tax itself.[21]

We have not yet mentioned the effect of the tax on people's *ability to work*. Clearly, the tax will not reduce the energy and ability of people with moderate or high incomes to engage in productive effort. However, the same cannot be said of those with incomes below the poverty line. Because a large number of low

[20] Joseph Pechman, *Federal Tax Policy* (Washington: The Brookings Institution, 1966), p. 63. (Reprinted by permission of the publisher) See also the discussion on pp. 71-73 of Chapter 5.
[21] It should also be noted that most of the nation's investment is done by corporations, whose tax rates, as we shall see, are lower than the income tax rates for high income people.

income people are required to give up part of their meager income in taxes, it is not unreasonable to speculate that the ability of these people to work effectively may be impaired.[22] To the extent that the tax reduces the disposable income of these families, it may deny them the quantity and quality of food, shelter, and clothing essential for the realization of work potential.

C. *Economic Stability*

The influence of a tax on the "ups" and "downs" in the level of economic activity is an important consideration in evaluating its worth. If a tax structure makes these ups and downs—inflations and recessions—more severe than they would otherwise be, the tax is said to be *destabilizing*. If it moderates the extremes of these fluctuations, the tax is *stabilizing*. Because the present income tax structure moderates these fluctuations with no necessary change in the tax law, it is called an *automatic stabilizer*.

To show how the income tax structure performs this stabilizing function, let us work through a simple example. Assume that an economy has 100 families, all of whom have two children and earn $5000 of income a year. The national income for this economy is, therefore, $500,000 (100 families × $5000). For each family, the amount of exempt income under the tax law is $600 per person, or a total of $2400. Assuming that each family has $600 of deductions, the taxable income of each family is $2000 ($5000 − $2400 − $600 = $2000). According to the schedule of rates in Table 7-1, each family would pay $290 of income tax, leaving each with $4710 of disposable income ($5000 − $290). For the whole economy, disposable income would be $471,000. It is out of this income that people spend. The higher the disposable income, the more they will spend on consumption.

[22] A recent study by the United States Treasury Department showed that, prior to the tax reform legislation of 1969, 6 percent of U.S. taxpayers with incomes below $3000 per year (a common poverty cut-off level) paid over 15 percent of their income in income taxes. This is to be contrasted with the 155 tax returns in 1967 with incomes over $200,000 on which *no* federal income tax was paid. One of the reforms in the 1969 legislation was to eliminate many of the nation's lowest income citizens from the federal tax rolls. Another was to impose a minimum tax on those with very high incomes. See U.S. Congress, House Committee on Ways and Means and Senate Committee on Finance, *Tax Reform Studies and Proposals, U.S. Treasury Department*, 1969, p. 80.

Now assume that the economy experiences a severe recession —national income falls 20 percent, from $500,000 to $400,000. Each family now has $4000 of income. Using the same procedure as above, the taxes paid by each family would fall by more than 50 percent—from $290 to $140. This would leave each family with disposable income of $3860 ($4000 − $140). The disposable income for the economy would be $386,000.

Notice now what has happened. While national income fell by $100,000, disposable income dropped from $471,000 to $386,000, or only $85,000. Because it is out of disposable income that people spend for consumption, spending will fall by less than is implied by the $100,000 drop in national income. Because it is spending that makes the economy "go," the effect of the income tax has been to reduce the recessionary forces at work in the economy. By maintaining spending at a higher level than it would otherwise have been, the income tax reduces the severity of the recession. Conversely, when the economy needs to be restrained, the tax structure, especially because it is progressive, tends to supply the needed restraint. It does so in this case by "soaking up" some additional income and automatically restraining consumption spending.

II. THE FEDERAL CORPORATION INCOME TAX

In addition to taxing the income of individuals and families, the federal government also taxes the income of corporations.[23] In recent years, this tax has accounted for about one-fifth of total federal tax revenue. While both the corporate and individual taxes are income taxes, the definition of income in each case is quite different. For the corporate tax, income is equivalent to *profit*. Consequently, the corporate tax is not a penalty for making sales, but is a penalty for being successful in operating the business.

---

[23] It should be noted that it is only the income of incorporated businesses which is taxed. Neither single proprietorships nor partnerships are covered by this tax law. Consequently, those industries which are dominated by the corporate form of business are more affected by this tax than are those industries which are characterized by noncorporate business. Earnings from single proprietorships and partnerships are covered by the personal income tax, however.

Table 7-3.   Income Statement of Corporation X and Calculation of Corporation Income Tax

Sales and other Revenue		$1,000,000
Total costs		− 800,000
Raw materials purchases	$400,000	
Wages	100,000	
Depreciation of building and equipment	150,000	
Rental payments	75,000	
Interest payments	25,000	
State and local taxes	50,000	
Profit before corporate tax (*taxable income*)		$ 200,000
Corporate income tax		
1st step—22 percent of first $25,000 of taxable income	$ 5,500	
2nd step—48 percent of remainder	84,000	
Total tax liability	$ 89,500	
Profit after corporate tax		$ 110,500

In Table 7-3, the income statement of a hypothetical corporation is shown and the calculation of the tax is derived. All of the numbers in this table up to the tax calculation are a normal part of every firm's income statement. From these data, the calculation of the tax is a simple matter. As in the personal income tax, the definition of *taxable income* is basic. In the corporate tax, taxable income is defined as the sales of the corporation minus the expenses which it incurs in doing business. These expenses or costs are itemized in Table 7-3 and include the costs of materials purchased from other businesses, wages, depreciation, interest, and rent. Having found its taxable income (profits before taxes), the corporation needs only to apply the corporation income tax rates. Again ignoring the presumably temporary surtax, corporate tax rates are 22 percent of the first $25,000 of taxable income and 48 percent of the rest. The lower rate on the first $25,000 of profit is designed to aid smaller corporations, some of which will not earn in excess of that amount.

The corporate tax is an indirect tax. In claiming a share of corporate profits, the government is taking income by indirect means from some group of persons. Unfortunately, it is terribly difficult to determine which people bear the burden of this tax. Three groups are candidates for the "bearer-of-the-tax" crown—

the owners of the corporations (stockholders), the employees of the corporation, and the people who buy the corporation's products. While there are reasons why each of the three groups might bear the tax burden, economic studies have been unable to resolve this issue definitively.

For example, it can be argued that the effect of the tax is simply to reduce the return on capital (or profits) of the corporation by about 50 percent, causing stockholders to realize only about one-half of the return which the capital invested in the corporation actually generates. According to this argument, the burden of the tax falls on the stockholders.

A second argument claims that the tax is shifted backwards onto the employees of the corporation. In this view, the tax is looked on by the corporation as an unavoidable cost which must be met. In attempting to minimize the impact of this cost on their profits, the corporation reduces other costs over which it has some control—for example, wage payments to labor. In this case, the burden of the tax falls on the workers who are employed by corporations. Moreover, in attempting to reduce labor costs, business firms may lay off some workers.

Finally, many (if not most) economists believe that (at least) some of the tax is shifted forward onto the buyers of the products produced by the corporation. Most corporations, it is argued, have some market power, some control over the price at which they sell. These firms set their prices so as to cover all costs and leave sufficient revenue for some predetermined rate of return. In order to preserve this rate of return, the corporate income tax gets included in the price and, hence, shifted forward onto buyers.[24]

While there is a logic to all of these positions, it appears that most economists find themselves more comfortable with the forward-shifting position than with the others. However, as we have noted, the evidence on this matter is not conclusive.

A. *Special Provisions*

While the corporate tax is less afflicted with special provisions than is the personal income tax, there are two special allowances

[24] In fact, it has been suggested that firms may use the tax as the lever by which to raise prices by more than the amount of the tax. If this is so, more than 100 percent of the tax may be shifted forward.

which deserve comment. These involve the definition and measurement of that deduction from gross income (sales) called "depreciation" and the special preferential treatment of the oil, gas, and minerals industries.

1. *Depreciation Allowance.* One of the most important expenses that is subtracted from sales to arrive at taxable income is that for depreciation of plant and equipment. During any period of time, plant and equipment used in production loses some value. This is so because it both wears out and grows obsolete. In Table 7-3, for example, a depreciation expense of $150,000 is recorded. Without question, the wearing out and obsolescence of equipment are legitimate production costs and are appropriately subtracted from sales to calculate profits (taxable income). This deduction differs from other expenses, however, largely because of its elusive nature and the difficulty of accurately measuring it.

A standard way of determining if the value of something has changed over time is to observe its market value when it is sold relative to when it was bought. The buildings, machines, and equipment owned by a business, however, are obviously not sold every year. Consequently, the estimation of how much their value changes—how much they depreciate—must be obtained in some other way. In practice, the estimation of depreciation expense is based on some rule-of-thumb procedure which experts agree is reasonable.

The simplest rule-of-thumb is to say that a machine (or other unit of capital) which lives 10 years loses 10 percent of its original value each year. This rule is called the straight-line method of depreciating assets. In practice, however, this procedure has become increasingly inadequate. One of the main reasons for its inadequacy is that when prices are rising in a period of inflation, the amount of value which is "recovered" from recorded depreciation expense is not sufficient to replace the worn-out machine or other asset. For example, consider a $1000 machine purchased in 1960 which will last 5 years. Because of inflation, the machine can be replaced in 1965 for no less than $1200. By the straight-line depreciation procedure, $200 of expense would be taken each year for a total recovery of $1000. This is inadequate to replace the machine; the company needs to recover $200 more in order to keep its productive capacity intact.

Because of the inadequacy of this method, corporations have argued for more liberal depreciation rules. Liberal in this context refers to procedures which would permit corporations to depreciate their assets at a faster rate. Rules more liberal than the straight-line method enable a corporation to deduct a greater volume of depreciation expense from each year's sales or gross income. This causes taxable income to be smaller which, in turn, reduces the corporation's tax liability. In both 1954 and 1963, the federal government recognized the legitimacy of some of these claims and more liberal depreciation procedures were adopted.

In addition to recognizing the legitimacy of the corporation claims, the government recognized that the level of investment in the economy could be influenced by adjusting the procedures for calculating depreciation. In particular, it was felt that economic growth could be encouraged by depreciation liberalization. If the rule of thumb for estimating depreciation became more liberal, depreciation allowances claimed by corporations would increase, taxable income and tax liability would decrease, and the corporation would have more after-tax profits than it would otherwise have had. Some of this additional profit would be used to purchase more capital equipment—hence, investment would rise and economic growth would be stimulated.[25]

The current procedures for calculating the corporation's depreciation expense, then, are a pragmatic compromise of attempts to represent accurately the value of capital "used-up" and to influence the level of the nation's investment and, hence, growth. Based on rules of thumb rather than objective evidence, depre-

---

[25] Much this same sort of reasoning was used to justify another special provision which was part of the corporation income tax law until 1969—the Investment Tax Credit. This provision was passed in 1962 and allowed a corporation to subtract 7 percent of much of the real capital investment which it undertook in a year from the amount of annual corporation tax which it would otherwise have had to pay. In effect, this provision meant that the federal government financed 7 percent of most new investments undertaken by corporations. Because this subsidy tended to stimulate investment and, hence, economic growth, it was judged a worthy provision when the economy was lagging and unemployment was high. During the inflationary period beginning in 1966, however, the investment tax credit was increasingly challenged and, in 1969, it was repealed as part of the tax reform legislation.

ciation expense is the "softest" deduction from sales in the calculation of corporate taxable income. As such, strong pressure for additional liberalization has persistently been applied by corporate business in searching for ways of reducing their tax liability.

2. *Mineral Depletion Allowance.* Although all corporate business is subject to the corporate income tax, a few industries have been singled out for preferred treatment. These are the oil and gas industries as well as some other extractive mineral industries. A special provision, called the *depletion allowance*, grants preferential treatment to these industries.

Early in the history of the corporation income tax, namely, 1918, the oil industry presented to Congress the argument that extractive industries were unlike others in that their "business" was to dispose of their very substance—the oil in the ground which they possessed. Congress responded by permitting these industries, in calculating their corporation tax, to deduct as an expense a certain percentage of their sales to cover the value of depleted oil reserves. For example, in calculating taxable income, the oil and gas industry may currently reduce their sales by 22 percent up to a limit of 50 percent of taxable income. Prior to the tax reform legislation of 1969, the allowance was 27.5 percent. Under the existing allowance then, the business in Table 7-3 could (if it were an oil company) subtract either $220,000 or 50 percent of taxable income (whichever is smaller) from gross sales in calculating its taxable income. Because the taxable income in the example is $200,000, the depletion allowance would permit $100,000 to be subtracted from sales *in addition to the other expenses*. The result would be to reduce taxable income from $200,000 to $100,000, leaving a total tax liability of $58,500. This is only slightly more than one-half of the original liability of $110,500 shown in the table.

From this example, it is clear that the depletion allowance grants enormous advantage to firms in extractive industries—especially the oil industry. In fact, this special provision reduces the taxes which extractive industries have to pay by over $1.25 billion per year. If federal revenue is to be maintained, other taxes have to be higher and other taxpayers have to pay $1.25 billion more taxes than they would otherwise.

Table 7-4. Profits, Taxes, and Taxes as a Percent of Profits of 10 of the Largest U.S. Oil Companies in 1968

Company	Net Profits Before Taxes ($ million)	U.S. Corporate Income Tax ($ million)	Taxes as a Percent of Profits
Standard (N.J.)	$2304	$234	9.7
Texaco	1019	24	2.4
Gulf	977	8	.8
Mobil	674	22	3.3
Standard (Calif.)	569	17	2.9
Standard (Ind.)	395	75	18.8
Shell	388	63	16.3
Atlantic-Richfield	240	3	1.2
Sun	228	44	19.4
Union	164	6	3.6
Total	$6958	$496	7.1

Source. Congressional Record, August 5, 1969, p. E6654.

The extent of the advantage provided to firms in the oil and other extractive industries is shown in Table 7-4.[26] On the basis of the stated tax rates, one would expect that the corporation income tax would, on the average, absorb at least 35 to 40 percent of a corporation's before-tax profits. In fact, in 1962, when corporation tax rates were at about the level they were in 1969, the tax absorbed over 42 percent of corporate profits. Table 7-4 shows the profits, the taxes paid, and the percent of profits absorbed by taxes for 10 of the largest oil companies in 1968. It is seen there that none of the oil companies paid more than 20 percent of their profits in taxes and that 6 of the 10 paid less than 4 percent of their profits in taxes. Two of the larger companies paid less than 2 percent. On the average, the 10 oil companies paid only slightly more than 7 percent of their net income (profits) in taxes. This is to be compared to the 40 percent rate paid by firms in non-oil or nonextractive industries.

Perhaps as serious as the redistribution of the tax burden caused

---

[26] It should be noted that these data refer to 1968, when the 27.5 percent allowance was still in effect. Under the current 22 percent depletion allowance, the percent of profits paid in taxes by oil companies would be increased, but only modestly.

by this provision is its effect on the allocation of the nation's resources. Because of the subsidized profits of firms in the oil and other extractive industries, capital in excess of the economic optimum is attracted to these activities. Insofar as the real return on investment in excess of the optimum is very low, the depletion allowance tends to reallocate the nation's capital from higher return uses outside the oil industry to lower return uses in it. For this reason, the overall productivity of capital in the U.S. economy is reduced. One manifestation of this misallocation of resources is the substantial excess capacity which exists in the oil and gas industries.

As is well known, the oil and other favored industries spend a great deal of energy and money to convince Congressmen and Senators of the wisdom and necessity of the depletion allowance. From time to time, it has been assailed in the Congress, but without major success. Former Senator Douglas has described his efforts to reduce this allowance as follows.[27]

Despite help from [two other members], we were periodically snowed under on the Finance Committee. Indeed, I sometimes suspected that the major qualification of most aspirants for membership on the Finance Committee was a secret pledge or agreement to defend the depletion allowance against all attacks. I suspected, also, that campaign funds reinforced these pledges.

Once again, we received little or no support from the Administration, which evidently thought the depletion allowance to be "too hot to handle." And, once again, the economics profession was largely silent, except for a few scattered voices that correctly pointed out that the tax favors led to overinvestment in the industry, thus causing the average return . . . on American investment to fall.

But there was little or no criticism from the economists of the morality of the tax advantage that helped a number of the fabulously wealthy to escape from paying any taxes whatsoever and helped many others to pay only nominal sums. There seemed to be no resentment among businesses that oil and gas companies only paid one-third to one-half the rate of taxation upon net profits paid by the main mass of American corporations. The prevailing sentiment seemed instead to be gratification that one group, at least, had been able to outwit the government and the reformers. Despite the fact that we wanted to lower the general tax rate once we had obtained greater uniformity in

[27] Paul Douglas, *op. cit.*, p. 30.

our tax system, and constantly stressed this point, we were about as popular among business executives as the revenue agents used to be among the mountaineers of Appalachia when they tried to put down "moonshining."

B. *Efficiency, Equity, and Stability*

Let us summarize the economic impacts of the corporation income tax. On efficiency and equity grounds, the corporate tax has been subject to far more criticism than the personal income tax.

While the personal income tax is more likely to affect the desire and ability of people to work as opposed to their desire and ability to invest, the corporate income tax is more likely to affect the latter. The effect of the tax on corporations' *willingness to invest* occurs because of the wedge which the corporate tax drives between the before-tax and after-tax rates of return on investments. For example, an investment which earns a 20 percent before-tax return yields only about a 10 percent after-tax return to the investor. The other 10 percent is paid in taxes. Because of this "tax bite," some investments that would be attractive in the absence of the tax are turned into unprofitable alternatives and are not undertaken. However, there is no solid evidence that the overall level of U.S. investment has been discouraged because of the existence of the tax. In addition, it should be noted that if the tax were shifted forward to buyers, the before-tax return would swell to include the tax leaving the after-tax or realized return the same as if there were no corporate income tax at all.

Similarly, it is reasonable to expect that the tax might reduce corporate *ability to invest*. Some have argued that, because corporations are required to share their profits with the government, they have fewer funds left over with which to replace plant and equipment or support expansion. However, since the adoption of the corporate tax, there have been other changes in the economy which have maintained the flow of investible funds to corporations at a high level. Among them are the capital gains provision of the personal income tax (which encourages corporations to use their profits to finance investment rather than pay them out in dividends) and, as we have seen, increasingly favorable depreciation provisions. Again, there is little evidence that corporations have been starved, or even squeezed, for investible funds.

In addition to its possible effects on the level of investment in the economy, the corporation income tax may have other economic efficiency or resource allocation consequences. The tax is, after all, a special tax on the profits of one form of business enterprise—the corporation. Consequently, it is reasonable to expect that the tax has induced a shift in investment away from corporation-dominated industries often characterized by large firms to those industries dominated by the typically small-sized single proprietorship and partnership form of business. Even if the tax were shifted forward, this reallocation would result. The prices of corporate produced goods would be higher and, because of downward sloping demand curves, the output of these industries would be reduced. No matter how the tax is shifted, resources would tend to be reallocated from corporate business to those sectors dominated by noncorporate enterprise.[28]

As was noted in our discussion of the tax-shifting phenomenon, the equity impact of the tax depends largely on the extent to which it is shifted and the direction of the shifting. To the extent that the tax is shifted forward, customers bear the tax burden; to the extent that it is shifted backward, laborers bear it; to the extent it is not shifted, the owners of the corporation—its stockholders—bear it. To estimate the progressiveness or the regressiveness of the tax, the income level of those individuals who ultimately bear the tax burden would have to be determined.

Finally, relative to the personal income tax, the corporate tax is only a modest built-in stabilizer. As we have seen, to be an automatic stabilizer, a tax must generate changes in consumption and investment spending which are in the opposite direction of the economy's movement. While corporate profits (and, therefore, also corporate taxes) change rapidly over the course of the business cycle—and in the right direction—the effect which these changes have on total spending in the economy is not likely to be large. This is so because the corporate income tax has only a marginal impact on both of the primary components of aggregate

[28] Implicit in the discussion of this paragraph is the assumption that the marginal tax rate paid on personal income by the owners of noncorporate businesses is less than the corporate income tax rate. Were this assumption not true, there would be no differential to induce a reallocation of resources away from corporations.

demand—consumption and investment spending. Consumption spending depends primarily on disposable income which is related to corporate profits only through the dividends which are paid out. Because corporations do not greatly alter their dividend payments even when profits fall, the influence of corporate profits and corporate profit taxes on consumption spending is not substantial. Moreover, investment spending depends far more heavily on *expectations* of future rather than current sales and profits. Consequently, even though corporate tax payments fall in a recession, the impact on the investment component of total spending is likely to be small.

III. OTHER FEDERAL TAXES

In addition to the personal and corporate income taxes, the other federal revenue sources include excise taxes, payroll taxes, and estate and gift taxes. Until recent years, these taxes played a relatively small role in the federal revenue structure. Recently, however, one of these taxes—the payroll tax—has assumed major importance in the tax structure. As social security benefits have been expanded, this tax, which finances the social security program, has also expanded.

A. *Payroll Taxes*

Federal payroll taxes are those imposed on the payment of wages and salaries. There are two basic types of payroll taxes—one which supports the unemployment insurance program and the other which supports the social security programs. We have seen that, because the revenues from these taxes go directly into special funds for these programs, they are called "earmarked taxes."

The payroll tax which supports the unemployment compensation program is levied only on employers. A second characteristic of the tax is that it is a flat-rate tax. Finally, the tax is paid only on the first $3000 of income earned by an employee. At the 3.1 percent tax rate prevailing in 1969, therefore, an employer would pay $93 (.031 × $3000) to the federal unemployment compensation trust fund for each of his employees who earned over $3000 per year.[29]

[29] For employers in many states, the tax rate can be reduced if the employer has maintained a stable employment record.

On the other hand, the payroll tax which finances the social security trust fund is levied on *both* employers and employees. As the benefit provisions of the social security program have become more extensive, the tax rates of this payroll tax have risen. In 1969, the tax rate was 4.4 percent and was levied on *both* the employer and the employee for the first $6600 of annual income. Consequently, for each wage earner making over $6600 per year, $290.40 (.044 × $6600) is paid into the social security trust fund by both the employer and the employee for a total of $580.80. As with the payroll tax for the unemployment compensation trust fund, the marginal tax rate for social security taxes falls to zero after a given level of income has been earned.

Because these taxes are levied either on employers or on both employers and employees, the total incidence of the tax is not easy to ascertain. The incidence of that portion of the social security tax which is levied directly on employees is clear—because it is deducted from employees' earnings, they bear the entire burden. However, the incidence of the portion of the tax paid by employers is more problematic. While some economists believe that this portion of payroll taxes is shifted forward to consumers in the form of higher prices, others judge that, in the long run, employees bear the burden of this portion of the tax also.

Clearly, the payroll tax levied on *employees* is a proportional tax up to the maximum income level. After this income level cut-off, the tax becomes seriously regressive. This is due to the zero marginal tax rate on these higher income levels. Similarly, if the employer-paid portion is shifted backwards onto employees, much the same sort of regressivity occurs at income levels above the cut-off. In one Treasury Department calculation assuming both backward and forward shifting, families earning $4000 to $7500 of income per year paid between 5.5 to 6 percent of their income in social security taxes, while families with over $15,000 annual income paid less than 3.2 percent of their income in taxes.[30] Clearly, this represents a serious regressivity pattern.

Because of this regressive nature of payroll taxes, the scheduled

[30] This study was cited in Pechman, *op. cit.*, p. 167. See also Table 6-2 where the degree of regressivity is estimated to be even more serious.

rapid expansion of the social security program will have serious consequences on lower income people. Their tax burdens will expand significantly. This effect has been described as follows.

When fully effective in 1987, the employee contribution for social security . . . will reach . . . $372.90 [for a person earning $6600]. This will exceed [1966 personal] income tax liabilities for . . . married persons with two children and incomes of $5,518. In 1966, the Federal payroll tax will be the highest tax paid by at least 25 percent of the Nation's [lowest] income recipients, and $350 million will be paid by persons officially classified as living below poverty levels.[31]

B. *Federal Excise Taxes*

Currently, the federal government levies excise taxes on liquor, tobacco, and gasoline. Because these are selective taxes, they tend to raise the price and reduce the consumption and production of the commodities on which they are imposed. The allocation of resources is, therefore, arbitrarily altered because of them.

As our analysis in Chapter 5 concluded, because an excise tax tends to raise the price of the commodity on which it is imposed, its burden is shared by both the producers and the consumers of the commodity. That is, the tax is partially shifted. Consequently, an excise tax (as a selective tax) discriminates against both the people who enjoy the taxed commodities and those who have capital invested in firms which produce these products.

C. *Estate and Gift Taxes*

As their name implies, these taxes are levied on bequeathed estates and gifts. While this form of taxation has substantial potential as a major revenue earner, existing United States tax legislation has incorporated so many special provisions that it is only a minor source of federal tax revenue.

IV. SUMMARY AND CONCLUSIONS

In this chapter, we have discussed in some detail the structure and effects of the federal tax system, especially the personal and corporate income taxes.

---

[31] *Ibid.*, pp. 167-168.

The personal income tax was observed to be the most comprehensive and largest revenue generator in the tax system. It is a direct, progressive tax which penalizes the earning of income. We noted the common presumptions concerning the impact of the tax on the willingness and ability to work and invest, but found evidence on these effects hard to come by. The structure of this tax includes many special provisions, most of which reduce the high stated tax rates on people with large incomes. The capital gains provision was viewed as an especially serious loophole.

The corporate income tax is a penalty imposed on the profitability of a particular form of business. Because of the lack of evidence on whether or not the tax is shifted and, if it is, in which direction, the equity impacts of this tax were difficult to determine. In general, this tax tends to discourage investment in corporations relative to noncorporations. This occurs because the tax may tend to reduce both the willingness and the ability of corporations to invest. The structure of this tax also has provisions which give preferential treatment to special groups. Of particular note is the percentage depletion allowance favoring the oil, gas, and other extractive industries.

One final comment appears in order. The special provisions built into the federal tax system may well have waste and inefficiency consequences which override any of the other impacts which we have mentioned. Because of the multitude of special provisions, the tax law gives opportunities for and, indeed, encourages behavior which reduces tax liability. In the United States, an enormous volume of energy is devoted to rearranging behavior and affairs so as to reduce the amount of taxes which must be paid. Indeed, there is a virtual "tax liability reduction industry" made up of bankers, accountants, lawyers, and professional trustees whose energies are devoted to searching for angles and special gimmicks to enable their clients to avoid paying taxes. From society's point of view, this effort represents a complete waste of resources that could be put to use producing something of real social value, be it steel or the services of doctors or teachers. This waste has been described in the following terms by former Senator Douglas.[32]

[32] Paul Douglas, *op. cit.*, p. 40.

The large hearing room of the Finance Committee seats a hundred and fifty persons. When we considered a tax bill, the room was filled with prosperous lawyers, graduates of great universities and of the top ranking law schools, whom Assistant Secretary of the Treasury Stanley Surrey once referred to in a burst of admiration as "the best minds in the country," all working to hold what they and their clients had and to enlarge it.

One major trouble with our tax system is, therefore, precisely this: that these "best minds" in the country have largely worked to make it what it is. Not more than one out of every hundred citizens actively working on a tax bill is trying to represent the general interest. And in the halls outside the hearing rooms the lobbyists are as thick as flies, while the publicity men and noisemakers are busily at work in Washington and elsewhere. In the halls of academe, erudite professors train their students in the intricacies of the tax code so that their students may succeed in the private practice of law by helping wealthy clients avoid taxes and thus beat the government of the people.

All this raises the question whether this is a fundamental weakness of our democratic system, namely, that the producing and possessing interests are compact, powerful, and well-organized, while the consuming and nonpossessing classes are busy with other things, and their interests diffused; and that while the people are numerically more numerous, they are collectively weak, ignorant and unorganized.

8

Public Expenditures—Considerations of Efficiency and Equity

Public spending affects the economy through many of the same linkages as does the imposition of taxes. The size and composition of public expenditures influence both the level of real national output and the distribution of this output among the people. In this chapter, we shall explore the economics of public expenditures at the federal government level. First, we shall inquire into the nature of the public expenditure decision process and discuss the role of economic analysis in making this process a more rational one. Then, a recent attempt to institute the systematic economic analysis of expenditure alternatives in the federal government will be described. Finally, we shall evaluate the desirability and feasibility of using the price system to distribute public outputs as opposed to the prevailing practice of giving them away.

I. THE FORMATION OF PUBLIC SPENDING DECISIONS

In Chapter 6, we discussed the structure of the budget-making process. In our discussion the full roster of performers in that scenario was introduced—the President, the executive agencies, the Bureau of the Budget, and the Congress (largely through its Appropriations Committees). That discussion focused on the formal budget and appropriation process. It cautiously skirted such difficult questions as: "Through what set of interacting forces is it decided that a manned lunar landing will be supported rather than federal aid to higher education?" Or, more generally, "By what machinations does the system of collective choice in a democracy generate budget allocation decisions?" "Are the expenditure decisions generated by this process likely to be in the public interest?"

To generalize about the process by which public expenditure decisions are made, we require a theory of government. We need a set of propositions which accurately describe the motivations of policy makers and the kinds of behavior that these motivations generate. Theorizing about government behavior (like theorizing about economics) is not a game which is restricted to a few select individuals. As any first course in political science will demonstrate, there are numerous theories of government with widely divergent emphases. In recent years, however, a sizable body of literature has appeared, all of which adopts a similar point of view on the motivation and behavior of government decision makers. This point of view appears to be increasingly accepted by political scientists and others interested in how public policy gets formed.[1]

For lack of a better name, we shall call this theory of government the *Self-Interested Policy-Maker Model*. This model hypothesizes that government decisions are formed through the interaction of the parties to decisions (policy makers), each of whom is attempting to advance *his own personal objectives* to the greatest extent possible. In many ways similar to the economist's theory of the utility-maximizing consumer or profit-maximizing businessman, this theory assumes that the people involved in public decisions—Congressmen, bureaucrats, Presidents, budgeteers, lobbyists—are rational strugglers each trying to further his personal interest by choosing the best available options. They are viewed as maximizing only one thing; their own *personal* net gain, their own *personal* utility. This theory, therefore, is an in-

[1] Some of the most significant items in this body of literature are James M. Buchanan and Gordon Tullock, *The Calculus of Consent* (Ann Arbor: University of Michigan Press, 1962), Anthony Downs, *An Economic Theory of Democracy* (New York: Harper and Row, 1957), and Roland McKean, "The Unseen Hand in Government," *American Economic Review,* June, 1965, pp. 496-505.

dividualistic theory—each participant in the game is only concerned with his own personal well-being and no one else's. The notion of the public servant guided by the "public interest" is emphatically rejected.[2]

It would not miss the mark by far to claim that this theory views the public policy maker as a rational, calculating, pain-pleasure machine. He lines up all of his alternatives, weighs the advantages and costs (to him) of each, and then chooses that option which leaves him better off than any other. While, obviously, a multitude of things may give him satisfaction—including material gain, favorable peer-group response, security, doing his job well, helping other people, getting reelected—the decision maker implicitly calculates gains and losses of each alternative so as to maximize his own, personal satisfaction from this many-dimensioned set of objectives.

Given that all public sector decision makers possess this self-interest characteristic, the process of public decision making (from forming the public budget to passing civil rights legislation) becomes clear. Because each person involved in a public decision has different objectives and different values, the outcome is the result of a *bargaining process*. Each participant haggles, using his influence and power, to reach a final outcome that is the most congenial to his personal interests. Indeed, influence and power become the "currency" with which the parties to a decision "buy" or "sell" in order to achieve the most personally congenial outcome. As has been documented in a number of studies, many public spending decisions can be explained as the outcome of a bargaining process which resolves an intricate and complex set of conflicting views and interests.

These propositions concerning the public decision process enable one to make much better sense of certain types of behavior displayed by policy makers. For example, according to this model, it is to be expected that those who are required to gain the support of others in order to exist would be very cautious about the positions that they take. One would expect them to be highly consul-

[2] This is not to say that a public servant never makes decisions that are in the public interest (whatever that means). It does, however, say that he will make decisions that are in the public interest only when they are also in his personal interest.

tative (in the sense of "touching all of the bases") prior to making a choice and extremely sensitive to the feelings of their constituents. This set of characteristics, for example, would apply to elected politicians, labor union leaders, corporation executives, and so on. For these people, the favorable reaction or support of followers, constituents, customers, employees, employers, and colleagues is an important (if not primary) component of those things which bestow satisfaction or utility rewards. To lose this favorable reaction or support is a satisfaction or utility penalty. The apparent dependence of such people on their constituents is quite consistent with this theory of public decision making. Indeed, the cautious and consultative behavior displayed by these individuals makes better sense in light of the theory.

Another aspect of observed behavior which jibes with the Self-Interested Policy-Maker Model is the influence on decision makers of the *probability* that any action that they take will have an effect. If the probability is high that his efforts will be successful, the decision maker is likely to expend a great deal of energy; low probabilities generate little effort. As one observer has stated:

> Everyone has an enormous stake in preventing thermo-nuclear war, but few persons put in several hours a day in efforts to prevent it. Why? Because they know that individual efforts of ordinary persons have almost no influence on the probability of such a war.[3]

This relationship of probability of success to effort expended is precisely what one would predict from the individualistic reward-penalty model. Low probabilities of success imply a high ratio of "energy cost" to success; high probabilities imply that success will come at low cost.

Another example: From the model one would expect that if the "price" (or cost) of achieving some objective would rise, the decision maker would opt for less achievement of that objective. Similarly, if its price falls, the decision maker would step up his efforts to achieve it—a sort of *Law of Demand* in political decisions. For example, if a Senator had to agree publicly to support colleague X in the next presidential election (the price or penalty) in order to obtain the award of a defense contract to a busi-

---

[3] Roland McKean, *Public Spending* (New York: McGraw-Hill, 1968), p. 15.

ness in his state, he would be less avid in seeking the contract than if he only had to commit his support for colleague X's pet water development project. Or, if the ardent supporter of civil rights legislation becomes President (and thus assumes control of the distribution of favors and patronage), the price (or cost) of a Congressman's initiating a filibuster on such legislation suddenly becomes very high. Because the price has risen, one would expect the Congressman to venture less opposition to such legislation than he might have otherwise. This behavior, also commonly observed, is consistent with—indeed, is anticipated by—the Self-Interested Policy-Maker Model and the bargaining process which it implies.

On the basis of this theory, economists and political scientists have drawn a number of analogues between the political decision process and the free and competitive market system. The competitive economic system, they suggest, leads to desirable results for the society because the practice of voluntary exchange forces individuals to bear the costs of actions which they take in order to reap private gain. Those who produce outputs can be compensated by imposing a price on those who desire the output. Those who use resources are required to compensate those who make the resources available. Through this kind of strict *quid pro quo* system, the goods and services people want most get produced and the public interest is served.[4]

According to the Self-Interested Policy-Maker Model, a similar *quid pro quo* bargaining mechanism develops in the public sector. Decision makers who gain personal satisfaction by successfully responding to the desires of their constituents engage in the political bargaining process. In this process, power and influence through the offering or withholding of political support is the currency. In order to gain something that provides benefit to those whose approval he cherishes, a public official is forced to commit his support on some other issue. This commitment is the cost which he must pay for the gain he realizes. If the relationship of the costs and gains that a policy maker bears approximate the relationship of the *social "harms"* and *social benefits* which his action generates, it can be argued that the political process oper-

[4] Recall the discussion in Chapter 2.

ates in the public interest in much the same way as does the competitive market economy. Both costs and benefits are accounted for in the decision process.

If this theory of government has merit, one can have some confidence that an ideal democratic political process does respond to the tastes and preferences of the people. The bargaining process which it implies reduces the coercive power which might otherwise be possessed by any group or segment of the society. It suggests, for example, that the wishes of minority groups will be appropriately accounted for—to ignore them would impose a real cost on individual decision makers in such an ideal bargaining process.

However, while the bargaining mechanism induced by rational, self-interested policy makers can, under ideal conditions, be presumed to guide public spending choices in line with the views of the people, some reservations should be offered. As in the case of the market system, this process operates in the public interest only if there are no imperfections or failures in the bargaining mechanism. Clearly, the political process in the United States is not such an ideal mechanism. Indeed, the failures in our political process are similar in nature to "market failures" in the private economy—externalities, lack of knowledge and information, monopoly power, cartelization, public goods, immobilities, and so on.

If the public sector bargaining mechanism manifests these imperfections, there will be a misallocation of resources (due to a misallocation of the public budget) in the same way that market failure in the private economy causes a misallocation of resources. In both cases, resource misallocation occurs because choices and decisions are made without all costs and gains being taken into account. Unworthy alternatives are chosen and, relative to the social optimum, too much or too little of certain things gets "produced."

While the results of private sector market imperfections are familiar (pollution, congestion, overproduction of some goods and underproduction of others, destruction of the natural environment), public sector spillovers, while fully as real, may be less widely recognized. For example, not all people's costs were reflected in the recent decision of the Public Health Service to dump 7500 gallons of sewage each day into Upper New York

Bay. Because of the failure of the bargaining mechanism to represent some people's interests, the decision to dump was not, in all likelihood, an optimal one.

Similarly, a local community, considering whether to provide excellent schools, is not likely to take into account the benefits which might be experienced by its next-door neighbor community in the case of a favorable decision.[5] To the extent that this spillover benefit is not reflected in the public expenditure decision, the decision is not likely to be optimal from the national point of view. Or again, because the Interior and Public Works Committees of the Congress are dominated by Senators and Congressmen from the South and the West, not all costs and gains get accounted for in the allocation of federal rivers and harbors appropriations.[6] Consequently, a number of public works invest-

---

[5] This kind of spillover effect is very important in discussions of state support for higher education. A state is not likely to provide optimal higher education services if it believes that many state university students will move to other states immediately after graduation.

[6] The following colloquy occurred in a recent hearing on the procedures for evaluating these projects.

Chairman Proxmire. We might as well be as blunt and comprehensive as we can on this. The problem is, we are not just dealing with sheer economic theory. We are dealing with some hard, tough political facts.

The people who really determine whether we go ahead with many of these projects are the members of the Senate and the House Interior Committees and the Secretary of the Interior. The President and Members of Congress have many, many other obligations and we tend to delegate to these gentlemen our decisions to a considerable extent in this area.

Look at the Interior Committee of the Senate and you will see that its members come from the following States: Washington, New Mexico, Nevada, Idaho, Alaska, Utah, North Dakota, Arizona, South Dakota, Wisconsin—I am happy to see there is one member from Wisconsin—Montana, California, Colorado, Idaho again, Arizona again, Wyoming, Oregon.

Practically all Western States. It is hard to find anyone from east of the Mississippi who ever serves on the Interior Committee.

Representative Moorhead. I might say to the Chairman, the same pattern holds in the other body.

Chairman Proxmire. Exactly.

So we have, you see, an atmosphere of bias, understandable bias, an atmosphere of political force here which I think we have to recognize.

U.S. Congress, Joint Economic Committee, Subcommittee on Economy in Government "Economic Analysis of Public Investment Decisions: Interest Rate Policy and Discounting Analysis," Hearings, 1968, pp. 37-38.

ments get undertaken which are not in the national interest. As one prominent observer put it:

> The costs and gains from the Arkansas River project [a notoriously inefficient undertaking] as viewed by its supporters must have diverged greatly from the total costs and gains as seen from the nation's viewpoint.[7]

In viewing the public spending decision process, then, it is helpful to keep in mind the bargaining mechanism implied by the Self-Interested Policy-Maker Model. This mechanism, if operating well, performs the same functions in the public decision process that the market system performs for the private economy. It tends to constrain private interests by imposing costs when harm is done to others. It provides the public spending process with a mechanism equivalent to Adam Smith's "invisible hand" in the competitive market economy. However, if operation of this mechanism is imperfect—if the costs and gains felt by certain people and groups are not represented in the bargaining process—the public interest will not be served. These imperfections cause undesirable public sector decisions in the same way that market failure causes misallocation of resources, waste, and nonoptimal private decisions.

II. PUBLIC SPENDING AND ECONOMIC ANALYSIS

We have argued that the bargaining process by which public spending decisions are made embodies a kind of invisible hand. This automatic guidance system insures that, in an effective political process, the full range of interests and tastes is represented when public decision makers pursue their own interest. In light of these assertions, one may question the role of economic analysis in the public spending process. If total benefits and total costs get automatically taken into account in the bargaining process, why should these impacts have to be specifically analyzed and estimated?

While not denying the importance of the bargaining process, we shall argue that economic analysis of public spending alternatives is a crucial step in securing good budget allocation deci-

[7] McKean, *op. cit.*, p. 27.

sions. The reasons for this assertion are not difficult to understand. First, the bargaining mechanism in the nation's public decision process is a highly imperfect one. Unrepresented interests and unaccounted-for costs and gains in the political system are, in all likelihood, more prevalent than "market failures" in the private economy—and some have argued that market imperfections are pervasive. In part, these imperfections in the bargaining process are caused by basic and deep-seated inadequacies in the United States political system.[8] However, to a large extent, they result from a lack of knowledge possessed by decision makers. Certain costs and gains fail to get accounted for in the decision process because they are not perceived. Decision makers and, indeed, beneficiaries may simply not be aware of the existence of the magnitude of certain kinds of gains or losses. Surely the bargaining process would be improved if the magnitude of the costs and benefits of various spending proposals and the distribution of these effects among the people could be accurately identified. Previously unrepresented beneficiaries and cost-bearers are much more difficult to ignore in the political process if their gains and losses are explicitly displayed before the decision maker. This information is precisely that which is generated by the economic analysis of public spending decisions.

A second reason for the economic analysis of public spending decisions relates to the inability of the bargaining process to distinguish economic from other kinds of effects. An ideal, smoothly functioning bargaining mechanism requires that the full range of society's values and objectives be reflected in decisions. These values range from economic efficiency to income distribution to moral positions against alcohol and drugs to deeply held feelings on questions of war and peace. Economic efficiency, it should be noted, is only one of these objectives. Even if the process is an effective one, it will not distinguish the extent to which a pro-

[8] One has only to mention a few of these to get the flavor of the argument: the tradition of Congressional seniority in combination with one-party systems in some regions which give certain (largely Southern and elderly) Congressmen and Senators quasi-permanent power; the overrepresentation of rural interests in the Congress; the ability of special interest groups to buy favors because of their wealth or their ability to hire able and numerous lobbyists; and so on.

posed expenditure contributes to the level of real economic welfare as opposed to other objectives. While the political process might well choose to undertake an economically inefficient expenditure in order to satisfy some other objective, it is essential to good decision making that the economic impacts be known with some precision. The participants to the bargaining process, for example, might well choose to undertake a large job-retraining program in the Watts area of Los Angeles, even if the economic returns to the nation are less than the economic cost of the program. The society may be willing to sacrifice some economic gain in order to obtain a reduction in the probability of civil unrest, some salve for its guilt of having failed for 300 years to provide equal opportunity for Negroes, or some contribution to neighborhood or family stability. In forming its decision, however, society should be aware of how much of economic gains it is giving up or trading off to attain these other objectives. Again, it is this information which the economic analysis of public spending proposals is able to yield.

Finally, the economic analysis of public expenditure alternatives is important because it forces all parties to a decision to focus on and debate the correct issues. If the inputs and the outputs of alternatives are spelled out, the values attached to them can be clearly debated—as indeed they should be. It is precisely these values which are debatable; it is precisely these values on which individual judgment may differ. The point is that the economic analysis of alternatives forces the debate to focus on these valuation issues, instead of on other matters that are not pertinent to securing choices in the public interest. Moreover, if the objectives which a decision is designed to achieve are clearly laid out and debated, decision makers are more likely to spread their net widely in searching for different, and better, ways of attaining objectives. As one writer put it: "The estimation of costs and benefits . . . virtually cries out for the examination of alternatives instead of the attempt to identify unique needs."

A. *Benefit-Cost Analysis—Some Basic Notions*

Accepting the importance of economic analysis to effective public expenditure decisions, let us explore some of the concepts and ideas used in evaluating public expenditures. We shall concentrate on a most basic technique of public expenditure evaluation known as *benefit-cost analysis.*

Considered in a most general way, benefit-cost analysis implies the challenging of every policy proposal with the question: "Do the gains to the people exceed the sacrifices required of them?" If the answer is affirmative, the proposal should be adopted; if it is negative, the proposal is not in the public interest. In this broad view of benefit-cost analysis, the theoretical framework of economics is employed, but precise measurement of gains and sacrifices may not be undertaken. Because of the informality of this sort of analysis, there is a tendency for the judgments of the analyst to get built into the evaluation, either implicitly or explicitly. While this kind of benefit-cost analysis is of substantial importance, its informality and its vulnerability to the analyst's prejudice are problems which should not be ignored.

Benefit-cost analysis considered more narrowly is also concerned with social gains and losses. It differs from broader policy analysis, however, in two primary ways. First, instead of utilizing the notions of economics only as a framework for sorting out relevant considerations, more formal benefit-cost analysis entails the quantitative estimation of the relevant variables, relationships, benefits, and costs. In this formal kind of analysis, objectives are specified, constraints stipulated, relationships established and quantified, and outcomes calculated—all with explicitness and openness.

Second, this narrower form of analysis requires deliberate efforts to exclude the personal values of the analyst. Formal benefit-cost analysis is premised on the proposition that the values which count are not those of the analyst, but rather the values held by the citizenry.[9] This kind of analysis, if applied to a proposed undertaking by two people with quite different personal values, would generate similar estimates of the economic impact.

In this more rigorous benefit-cost analysis, the calculation of a benefit-cost ratio is often the end result of the study. The *numerator* of this ratio is defined as the *present value*[10] (expressed

[9] Such values, for example, are those reflected in the prices for which goods and services are exchanged in the market economy.

[10] The phrase "present value" is used to emphasize that it is the value of benefits as they appear at a point in time—the present—which is of rele-

in dollars) of all of the expected economic benefits attributable to a proposed undertaking. The monetary values or prices which are attached to these benefits are those which society has placed on them as observed in (or inferred from) private sector markets.

The *denominator* of the benefit-cost ratio is defined as the *present value* (expressed in dollars) of the costs of undertaking and operating the project. If it is a large capital investment project (a highway or a dam, for example), costs are composed of two types—capital (or construction) costs and operation, maintenance and repair costs. Capital costs are those which occur before the project begins producing output. The remaining costs (for operating, maintenance, and repair) are future expenses—those which occur after the project is operating.

On the basis of these definitions, the benefit-cost ratio (Z) is defined as the ratio of the *value* of the benefits of a program to the *value* of the program's costs:

$$Z = \frac{\text{present value of economic benefits}}{\text{present value of economic costs}}.$$

Clearly, if the ratio is greater than one, public expenditures for the project are judged to be economically worthwhile. If it is equal to one, the public expenditure adds nothing, on balance, to the nation's economic welfare; if it is below one, it detracts from economic well-being.[11]

It should be emphasized that the values in both the numerator and denominator of the ratio are *economic* benefits and *economic* costs. Although they are measured in dollars, all impacts, including spillovers and externalities, are included. The calculation of the benefit-cost ratio, therefore, requires a kind of social accounting which is significantly different from that used by the businessman who is evaluating a proposed private sector investment.

This formal type of benefit-cost analysis serves three purposes for the public decision maker. It assists him in (1) developing the

vance. Benefits (and costs) have to be appraised at a point in time because, for many projects, benefits are produced and costs incurred over a long period of time. We shall investigate this present value concept in greater detail in the next section.

[11] The concept of the benefit-cost ratio and some problems encountered in measuring benefits and costs are discussed in the next section.

optimum size program or project, (2) designing the program to be of maximum efficiency, and (3) choosing from among the alternatives open to him the set of options that is the most productive.

The problem of developing a particular program or project to best achieve explicit and well-defined objectives involves the first two considerations. Not only does the optimal size of the program or project have to be determined, but also the available inputs have to be combined in the most efficient way—so that they yield the most output (benefit) for any cost. These two aspects of an economic public spending program can be visualized in Figure 8-1. The size of an undertaking—measured in dollars of cost—is plotted on the horizontal axis of that diagram. The vertical axis shows the value of both the outputs and the inputs, also expressed in dollars. Because both axes measure dollars of cost, the curve displaying total cost is the 45° line labeled *TC*. The total amount of benefits *from a most efficiently designed project of each possible size* is shown by the curve labeled TB. Its shape is consistent with the Law of Diminishing Returns. From the diagram, it is seen that at project size *A*, total benefits of an efficiently designed project are *AB*, total costs are *AC*, and the benefit-cost ratio is *AB/AC*. Similarly, the benefit-cost ratios of project sizes *D*, *G*, and *I* are *DE/DF*, *GH/GH* = 1, and *GK/GJ*. For project sizes *D*, *G*, and *I*, the benefit-cost ratios are, respectively, greater than one, equal to one, and less than one.[12]

If the decision maker can undertake as many projects or programs as are efficient, benefit-cost analysis can be of assistance in choosing the optimal *size* project. Assume for a moment that project sizes of *A*, *D*, *G*, and *I* are the *only* possible sizes. The question is: Which size is the best? Clearly, size *I* can be ruled out—the present value of its costs exceed the present value of its benefits. Similarly, size *G* can be excluded. Because benefits just equal costs, the program is a no-net-gain proposition. Society would be just as well off without the program as with it.

Sizes *A* and *D*, however, are not so easily disposed of. Except

12 It should be noted that the terms "benefits" and "costs" in this discussion and in Figure 8-1 are properly interpreted as "present value of benefits" and "present value of costs."

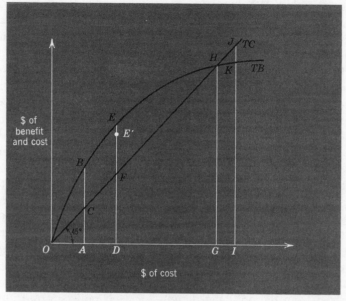

Figure 8-1

that they are mutually exclusive options (if you choose one size, you cannot choose the other), both would be worthwhile ventures. Benefits exceed costs in each case. It is with respect to such choices that the marginal principle so basic to economics must be consulted. This principle specifies that *inputs should continue to be added so long as the last dollar of cost generates more than a dollar of benefits*—so long as marginal benefit exceeds marginal cost. The optimal size of the project occurs where marginal benefit equals marginal cost ($MB = MC$). A corollary of this principle is that the optimal project size is attained when the excess of benefits over costs (total benefits minus total costs) is the greatest.[13] In our example (in which we have to choose between sizes A and D), the optimal size is D—at D the *excess* of benefits over costs (EF) is greater than the *excess* of benefits over costs at size A (BC). Indeed, as our diagram has been drawn, there is no size along the horizontal axis for which the excess of benefits over costs

[13] Recall our more detailed discussion of this principle in Chapters 4 and 5.

is greater than *EF*. At size *D*, marginal benefit equals marginal cost and total benefits minus total costs are as great as possible.[14]

Benefit-cost comparisons are also helpful in planning the most efficient project at any given size. No matter what size project is ultimately decided on, an optimal design requires that the most benefits get produced for the cost which is incurred. For example, assume that project size *D* (Figure 8-1) has been selected. Given this project size, economic efficiency considerations demand that the total benefits produced by this size project be maximized. In all likelihood, there are a number of ways to design a project of size *D*. Each of these designs will generate a given volume of benefits. One of these alternative designs, for example, might generate benefits of *DE'*. Another might generate benefits of *DE*. The question which benefit-cost comparisons can assist in answering, then, is the following. Which of the possible project designs for any given size is the optimal—which design yields the greatest stream of benefits? Clearly, the decision maker would attempt to choose the design that is on the *TB* curve, since this curve is derived from the optimum designs for each project size. In our example, this is the design yielding *DE* of benefits.

From this discussion, it is clear that benefit-cost calculations are important in both the design of a project and the choice of its size. However, because the planner cannot know the optimum size without knowing the results of a number of designs, these two decisions are interdependent. Indeed, the optimum size and design combination can be determined only after rather comprehensive benefit-cost calculations. For example, it is the *TB* curve that determines the *optimum size* project. However, this curve is not known until the *most efficient design* for each project size has been found. The optimum size-optimum design combination

14 It should be noted, however, that while project *D* is the optimum size project, there are a number of project sizes which have greater benefit-cost ratios than it. In fact, project size *A* has a benefit-cost ratio, *AB/AC*, which exceeds project *D*'s ratio *DE/DF*. For finding optimum project size, then, the appropriate criterion is *maximum net benefits* (total benefits minus total costs) and not the maximum benefit-cost ratio. To determine project or program size by picking the size with the highest benefit-cost ratio would lead to the wrong choice.

can be simultaneously arrived at with the assistance of benefit-cost calculations.

Finally, in addition to guiding project size and design decisions, benefit-cost analysis is also of assistance in choosing among worthwhile alternative projects, if all of them cannot be undertaken simultaneously. For example, assume that in the Department of Health, Education, and Welfare, the decision maker has $1 million which can be allocated to health programs this year and that he is confronted with the five alternative public health projects shown in Table 8-1. All of these projects, it will be noted, have

Table 8-1. Five Alternative Health Projects and Their Benefit and Cost Characteristics

Project	Present Value of Costs	Present Value of Benefits	B/C
A	$250,000	$400,000	1.6
B	250,000	400,000	1.6
C	250,000	500,000	2.0
D	250,000	300,000	1.2
E	250,000	360,000	1.44

benefit-cost ratios greater than one. To simplify the analysis, assume that each project costs $250,000, all of which comes out of this year's budget.

The question is: Which four of the five projects should be undertaken? Again, the criterion cited earlier is the relevant one. One should choose so as to obtain the greatest net benefits (total benefits minus total costs). However, in the case of deciding from among a set of alternative projects (as opposed to determining the optimum program design or size), the benefit-cost ratio is a good guide. Net benefits will be maximized if the decision maker ranks the projects by their benefit-cost ratio (from highest to lowest) and moves down the list until his budget is exhausted.[15] Following this rule, the five projects of Table 8-1 would be ranked

[15] In this exercise, we have omitted an interdependence which would have to be considered in the performance of actual benefit-cost analysis. This is the interdependence between the size of the budget (if it is limited) and the optimum project design and size.

C, A, B, E, D and, of the five, those four with the highest benefit-cost ratios would be chosen (C, A, B, and E).

Benefit-cost calculations and the maximum net benefit criterion, then, can assist the decision maker in choosing among alternative project designs, project sizes, and discrete projects with different purposes. From these calculations, the decision maker can understand the economic gains and costs involved in his choices and, moreover, can clearly see how much economic efficiency will be sacrificed if choices are made to satisfy other objectives that are not represented in the benefit-cost calculations.

In this discussion of benefit-cost analysis we have argued a number of propositions. These are summarized in the following points.

1. Benefit-cost analysis is a tool of the decision maker; its function is to generate information on the economic effects of alternative public expenditure decisions and to assist the decision maker in his search for the set of alternatives that generates the greatest net benefit. In focusing discussion on the economic benefits and costs of alternatives, this kind of analysis improves the political decision process. It uncovers gains and losses which might otherwise be neglected in the bargaining mechanism and encourages decision makers to undertake a comprehensive search for alternative means of attaining an objective.

2. Social values are employed in formal benefit-cost analysis and are "discovered" by referring to observed prices in private markets. Where private markets are imperfect, observed prices may have to be adjusted. By relying on the values that are or would be generated by markets, the value judgments of the analyst are minimized.

3. Formal benefit-cost analysis is helpful in decisions on project size, project design, and the choice among alternative projects when the budget is limited. Because these decisions are interdependent and because the benefits of alternative projects are often interdependent, formal benefit-cost calculations must be based on systematic analysis and models which make explicit all of the relevant interdependencies and relationships.

4. It is essential that the benefit-cost criterion—maximum net benefits—be followed in order to attain economic efficiency in

public expenditure decisions. This criterion presumes that the goal of gaining the greatest value of output for the resources used is a significant social objective. It is not formally concerned with other matters which are also of social concern—the distribution of the output and costs among various groups and people, the movement of people from location to location, the alteration of deeply held values, the rate of population growth, and so on. Because benefit-cost analysis guides public sector decisions by comparing the dollar value of outputs and inputs, these other objectives, which cannot be valued in dollars, are not handled neatly in the benefit-cost framework. The public decision maker, however, must be sensitive to defining these other things as explicitly as possible and insuring that they do get included in the decision process.

B. *Benefit-Cost Analysis—Some Problems of Implementation*[16]

In our discussion of benefit-cost analysis in the previous section, we avoided some of the more difficult matters involved in evaluating the worth of alternative public expenditures. In this section, we shall discuss three significant, partially unresolved issues dealing with the accurate measurement of the economic effects of public expenditures. These problems are (1) the treatment of time; (2) the valuing of inputs and outputs when markets are imperfect; and (3) the incorporation into benefit-cost analysis of social objectives other than the basic economic efficiency objective.[17]

1. *The Treatment of Time.* One of the primary applications of benefit-cost analysis is in evaluating the worth of long-lived public undertakings—investment programs which produce outputs for many years into the future and whose operation entails costs in future years. An example of such a public investment undertaking is the construction of a large dam to control floods.

A significant problem arises in evaluating public investments

[16] This section deals with some fairly advanced problems in benefit-cost analysis. It can be omitted with no loss of continuity.
[17] See Robert H. Haveman and Julius Margolis, eds., *Public Expenditures and Policy Analysis* (Chicago: Markham Publishing Co., 1970), for further analysis and discussion of these matters.

because of the different time periods in which benefits and costs are experienced. This problem exists because of a very basic proposition: *A dollar of benefits (or costs) not expected until next year, is worth less than a dollar of benefits (or costs) expected today.* That is to say, time matters. The value of a thing depends on *when* one will gain use of it—a dollar has a specific value only at a specific date. Thus, a dollar placed in a savings account a year ago has become $1.05 today (at 5 percent interest per year) and will become $1.1025 next year. Likewise, a dollar not expected until next year is worth about 95¢ today if the interest rate is 5 percent. A dollar's value is a function of (depends on) time.

In benefit-cost analysis, both inputs and outputs are valued in terms of dollars—a common unit of account—so that benefits and costs can be compared and decisions can be based on the outcome. When time matters, the money unit by which we value inputs and outputs becomes a rubber yardstick. Dollars are no longer equal to dollars. To be accurate, then, we must not only state inputs and outputs in terms of dollars, but we must state them in terms of dollars of the same date.

It has become common practice to measure all future benefits and costs in terms of *today's dollars.* This makes sense because decisions must be made today between both alternatives which have no future benefits and costs and alternatives which do. To compare these alternatives, both present and future benefits and costs are stated in terms of their *present value.*[18]

---

[18] From our discussion of the effect of time on values, it is clear that if receiving $1 of income is deferred, its *present value* is less than $1. Conversely, if I have $1 today, I can turn it into more than $1 in a future year by loaning it at some rate of interest. For example, if the interest rate is 5 percent, I can turn the dollar I hold today into $1.05 a year from today. However, if I expect to receive $1.05 a year from today, the *present value* of that $1.05 is about $1. A simple formula for this is

$$P(1 + r) = F_1 \qquad (1)$$

in which P is the present value, r is the rate of interest, and F_1 is the amount received one year in the future. For example, if I have $1 today ($P$) and if the interest rate (r) is 10 percent (or .10), the $1 can be turned into $1.10 ($F$) a year from today: (*continued on page 159*)

In symbolic terms, the numerator of the benefit-cost ratio—the *present value of the stream of benefits*—is stated:

$$\sum \frac{B_t}{(1 + r)^t},$$

in which $\sum$ means "summation over all the years," B_t stands for the benefits expected in the tth year, and $(1 + r)$ is the discounting factor by which values expected in the future are turned into today's values. Similarly, the denominator of the benefit-cost ratio—the *present value of capital and future operation costs*—is stated:

$$K + \sum \frac{O_t}{(1 + r)^t},$$

in which K is the capital or construction costs (assumed to occur in the current year) and O_t are the operation, maintenance, and

---

$$\$1 \ (1.10) = \$1.10. \tag{2}$$

If I keep my \$1 invested at 10 percent for 2 years, it turns into \$1.21. This is determined by going through the same calculation two times:

$$\$1 \ (1.10) \ (1.10) = \$1.21 \tag{3}$$

While the formulae above are correct for calculating the future value of something owned today, they are awkward for going in the other direction —for calculating the present value of something not expected until the future. The formulae can be easily revised to go from future to present values as follows:

$$P = \frac{F_1}{1 + r} \tag{4}$$

and

$$P = \frac{F_t}{(1 + r)^t}. \tag{5}$$

The second of these formulae reads: The *present value* (P) of some amount expected in year t (F_t) is $\dfrac{F_t}{(1 + r)^t}$ when the interest rate is r percent. This process of calculating present values is called *discounting*.

repair costs expected in the tth year. The full benefit-cost ratio
(Z) is stated as:

$$Z = \frac{\sum \dfrac{B_t}{(1+r)^t}}{K + \sum \dfrac{O_t}{(1+r)^t}};$$

the ratio of the present value of the benefits over the present value
of capital plus future operation costs.[19]

We have noted that the procedure used to calculate present
values is called *discounting*. From our description of this process
in footnote 18, it is clear that the size of the interest rate used to
do discounting is very important. The effect of the interest rate on
benefit-cost calculations has been described as follows in a recent
Congressional report. The present value of benefits and costs
shown there were calculated from formulae like those presented
in the last paragraph.

The following table presents a simple example of the impact of the
discounting procedure on the economic evaluation of an investment.

*The Effect of Discounting on the Evaluation of a Typical Investment,
Using Discount Rates of 0, 3, 5, and 10 percent* [Dollar Amounts in Thousands]

	Interest rate (in percent)			
	0	3	5	10
Value today [present value] of total benefits	$15,000	$10,448	$8,456	$5,442
Value today [present value] of total costs	7,500	6,741	6,409	5,906
Benefit-cost ratio	2.00	1.45	1.32	0.92
Value today [present value] of excess of benefits over costs	7,500	3,707	2,047	−468

[19] These present value formulae, it should be noted, are very close to formula 5 in footnote 18. The main difference is that the formulae in the text have a summation sign (Σ) in them. This has to be there because formula 5 in footnote 18 gives the present value (P) for some single-shot value expected in year t (F_t). Most government projects have benefits which occur in each year for a number of future years. The formulae in the text, then, say that the present value of these future benefits must be added together to get the total present value of the stream of benefits.

Investment X is expected to cost $5 million next year. The project is expected to yield benefits or revenues of $600,000 per year for the next 25 years which if simply added up, total $15 million. It requires the continued expenditure of $100,000 per year to keep it in operation.

From the calculation displayed in the table, the necessity for accurate and consistent discounting is clear. The expected benefit-cost ratio of the example project is 2 if no discounting is applied. The ratio drops to 1.3 with an interest rate of 5 percent and to below unity with a rate of 10 percent. If the costs and benefits are added with no account taken of the time factor, the project shows an excess of benefits over costs of $7.5 million. If an interest rate of 10 percent is applied, costs are estimated to *exceed* benefits by nearly $0.5 million.[20]

From this description, it is apparent that the size of the interest rate that is used in discounting analysis is of crucial importance. The higher this rate, the fewer projects which will show a benefit-cost ratio greater than one. The higher the rate, the more difficult it is for projects whose outputs occur far into the future to generate a favorable benefit-cost ratio.

Economists and others concerned with benefit-cost practices have long debated the size of the appropriate public interest rate for discounting analysis. The range of positions on this matter is, in large measure, a result of imperfections in our market economy. Because of these imperfections, a large number of interest rates can be observed at which people borrow and lend instead of a single rate of interest. Similarly, observed profit rates extend from very high to very low, signaling a wide range in the productivity of capital in the private sector.

Most observers now agree that the government, in pursuing national economic efficiency, should undertake no expenditure which earns a smaller return than the same resources would earn in an alternative use. Because the resources used by the government would be alternatively used in the private sector, the government must look to private interest and profit rates to determine the appropriate public interest rate for discounting. This position reflects the application of the basic "opportunity cost" principle—the cost of the resources used by the government is equal to the loss of the value which these resources would

[20] U.S. Congress, Joint Economic Committee, "Economic Analysis of Public Expenditure Decisions: Interest Rate Policy for Discounting Analysis," Report of the Subcommittee on Economy in Government, 1968, pp. 5-6.

otherwise produce.[21] This principle was reflected in the government report referred to earlier:

> [P]rivate citizens should not, in general, be forced to give up a portion of their incomes in the form of higher taxes to support public undertakings which are of less social value than the uses to which their funds would otherwise be put. The way for the Federal Government to assure this result is to adopt in public investment appraisal an interest rate policy which reflects the private sector opportunities forgone.[22]

This opportunity cost interest rate has been in the 8 to 10 percent range during the decade of the 1960s. The government should be using an interest rate of this magnitude in discounting future benefits and costs.[23]

2. *Valuing with Imperfect or Nonexistent Markets.* We have seen that it is important that a standard yardstick be applied in comparing the social value of the resources consumed by a public program (costs) and the social value of the outputs which the expenditure generates (benefits). We have claimed that dollars can serve as this standard unit of account. Moreover, it has been argued that the market prices observed in the private economy are, under most circumstances, good indicators of social value. By attaching these prices to program inputs, costs—taken to mean the amount that those who furnish the inputs would require to make them feel justly compensated—are accurately measured. Similarly, benefits are accurately measured by valuing project outputs at observed market prices.

If all of the markets in the economy were competitive, functioning effectively, and comprehensive, prices for all outputs and inputs would be available and reliable. These estimators of economic values could be plucked from the appropriate markets and

---

[21] There are, however, some who argue that observed interest or profit rates provide little guidance in obtaining a public discount rate. Among other things, they claim that existing private sector rates do not reflect the *collective* willingness of people to provide for future generations in their private decisions. These economists, in effect, view "providing for the future" as a public good and, hence, not produced in sufficient quantity through individual private decisions.

[22] U.S. Congress, Joint Economic Committee, *op. cit.*, pp. 12-13.

[23] It should be noted that this is substantially higher than the 4 to 5 percent rates which are now used in many government benefit-cost analyses.

directly attached to the inputs and outputs of public expenditure programs. The practical implementation of benefit-cost analysis would be greatly eased.

Unfortunately, however, markets are not these smoothly functioning organisms, and when they are imperfect, observed prices fail to reflect social values accurately. In Chapters 2 and 3, we catalogued the prominent market imperfections and failures and described them in some detail. As will be recalled, these imperfections run the gamut from monopoly power to immobilities to externalities or spillovers to lack of market information. Moreover, we noted the limitation on the significance of observed prices due to their dependence on a particular, less-than-ideal distribution of income. Because of the market imperfections and the income distribution consideration, many prices observed in the real world are not reliable and must be "corrected" in doing benefit-cost analysis. The process of adjusting faulty market observations is called *shadow pricing*.

The task of developing appropriate rules for adjusting observed prices is not an easy one. There are no obvious guides to determining social values once the relatively firm ground of market observations becomes unreliable. Because of this lack of guidance, some have felt that the prospects for developing meaningful indicators of social values when markets are imperfect are not good. They argue that the research designed to generate these values has not been terribly productive and that where externalities or public goods are present, markets may be nonexistent, let alone imperfect.

One interpretation of this position is that benefit-cost analysis must simply use and live with these imperfect, observed prices. It is claimed that in so doing, decision makers will have to focus on these valuation matters. The political process will be forced to make deliberate judgments on these values. Another option would be for "cost-effectiveness" analysis to be substituted for benefit-cost analysis. With this method, benefits are not measured and objectives are only described. The task of analysis in this case is to minimize the value of resources used (costs) to attain the stated objective.[24]

---

[24] This is the kind of analysis that has been employed in the Department of Defense where decisions must be made on expenditures that produce true

Most benefit-cost analysts, however, are not this gloomy. They argue that the immediate solution of these problems should not be expected. The application of benefit-cost analysis is as yet in its infancy. These experts also point out that research efforts to obtain shadow prices[25] have produced results which are significantly more helpful to the decision maker than unstudied assertions or *ad hoc* judgments. These estimation efforts, it is noted, need result in only a miniscule increase in the efficiency of a program to justify their cost.

In support of this latter position, it should be emphasized that analysts confronting imperfect market prices are not without clues as to the direction in which the shadow price diverges from the observed price or the extent of the divergence. Indeed, knowledge of market structure and performance provides substantial guidance for shadow pricing. If, for example, monopoly exists in a market, one can safely assume that the observed price must be adjusted downward, and knowledge of costs and profits gives some basis for the size of the adjustment. If, because of a government price support program, there is significant overproduction of, say, an agricultural commodity, its observed price clearly overstates the social value of additional production. The analyst is justified in assigning it a price of zero if the additional output of this commodity will not be utilized. Or, again, if the economy is not fully employed, the market wage of laborers which would otherwise be unemployed overstates the cost to the economy of the government's using them. Knowledge of their alternative use provides a basis for adjusting downward their market price in calculating the appropriate shadow value.

This more optimistic position argues that if markets are imperfect and observed prices unreliable, it is more important for decision makers to have synthetic prices which are reasonable estimates of social values than to base public decisions on er-

---

public goods. It is likely to be impossible ever to measure the value of the benefits of providing national defense.

[25] A shadow price could be defined most simply as a synthetic value attached to a unit of input or output which represents the social value of the item used up or produced. As we have emphasized, these synthetic values are necessary when there is no market observation or when there is reason to believe that the observed price does not represent social value.

roneous prices, even though they are observed. To those who emphasize the difficulty and the absence of any guidelines for estimating shadow prices, one analyst has replied:

In short, what is tangible or intangible, measurable or immeasurable, is less a matter of what is abstractly possible than it is of what is pragmatically, and at reasonable cost, feasible. In the Middle Ages and earlier, it must surely have been argued by some that one's feeling of warmth or cold was intangible, unmeasurable and so on. Fortunately, Gabriel Fahrenheit did not agree.[26]

3. *Valuing with Multiple Objectives.* Our discussion so far has assumed that the estimation of social benefits and costs would be a simple matter if only smoothly functioning markets existed for all of the inputs and the outputs of government programs or if appropriate shadow prices could be derived. Some, however, would not go this far. While admitting that appropriate prices enable accurate estimates of a program's *economic* impacts, they point out that the government has other objectives which are not economic. In recent discussions the equity or income redistribution objective has been at the heart of the debate. It is noted that market prices depend on the pattern of demands which, in turn, depend on the distribution of the nation's income. Because one of the government's basic responsibilities is to alter the nation's income distribution, it is argued that analysts should not use observed prices determined by an income distribution which the government implicitly rejects.

If equity considerations are important, this argument continues, the government should make an explicit judgment that income going to some people is more important than income accruing to others. The practice of using market prices neglects this judgment. It assumes that a dollar's worth of income is a dollar's worth of income, irrespective of who gets it or who gives it up. If equity considerations are to count, the government should place different weights on dollars of benefits and costs depending on who gets them or who bears them. These weights should represent the government's judgment on the way in which the distribution of

[26] Burton Weisbrod, "Concepts of Benefits and Costs," in Samuel B. Chase, Jr., ed., *Problems in Public Expenditure Analysis* (Washington: The Brookings Institution, 1968) p. 261.

income ought to be altered. They should be determined through the political process and consistently applied in the evaluation of all public expenditures.

As an example of how this "welfare weighting" proposal would be implemented, consider a public project for which the present value of benefits is $1.5 million and the present value of costs is $1.0 million, yielding a benefit-cost ratio of 1.5. The way in which the benefits and costs of this project are distributed among people of various income levels is shown in Table 8-2. In the second column, the distribution of the benefits of the project is shown; the distribution of project costs is shown in the fourth column. While the outputs tend to be received by the higher income classes, the bulk of the costs are borne by people in the lowest income category.

Assume that in fulfilling its mandate to secure equity by re-distributing income, the government attached the weights shown in the first column of the table to increases (decreases) of income to people in the various income classes. Dollars of income going to or coming from those in the lowest income class are given a weight of 1.5; dollars of income to or from people in the highest class are given a weight of .8. The dollar values of both benefits and costs can now be adjusted by multiplying them by the weights. Columns 3 and 5 present the weighted benefits and costs to each of the income groups. While total unweighted benefits are $1.5 million, total weighted benefits are calculated to be $1.53 million. Unweighted costs of $1 million are adjusted to $1.38 million. Because of the "adverse" distribution of benefits and costs—benefits going primarily to the well-to-do and costs levied largely on the poor—the unweighted benefit-cost ratio of 1.5 ($1.5 million/$1.0 million) is reduced to a weighted ratio of 1.11 ($1.53 million/$1.38 million).

Were this sort of calculation performed on all public spending alternatives, those that favored lower income groups would have their benefit-cost ratio raised relative to those that favored the higher income groups. Consequently, if the budget were allocated by moving from the projects with higher benefit-cost ratios to projects with lower ratios, poorer individuals and regions would tend to be favored in the budget allocation relative to high income individuals and regions.

Table 8-2. Redistribution Weights and the Distribution of Project Benefits and Costs by Income Class

Income Class (in dollars)	(1) Weights	(2) Distribution of Benefits	(3) Weighted Benefits	(4) Distribution of Costs	(5) Weighted Costs
$ 0–3000	1.5	$ 300,000	$ 450,000	$ 800,000	$1,200,000
3000–7000	1.0	600,000	600,000	100,000	100,000
7000 or more	.8	600,000	480,000	100,000	80,000
Total		$1,500,000	$1,530,000	$1,000,000	$1,380,000

Like the other issues raised in this section, the treatment of multiple objectives in public expenditure evaluation has not been resolved among those who theorize about or apply benefit-cost analysis. A number of points raised in the discussion of this issue should be mentioned, however. For one thing, it has been pointed out that there are a number of government activities which are undertaken for a strict productivity or economic efficiency purpose. These activities, like building dams or laying highways, are not undertaken to redistribute income but, instead, to provide a service that the private sector cannot provide—to correct for market failure. Because of their limited economic purpose, it is claimed that these activities should not be designed to serve other, nonefficiency objectives.

A second point concerns the difficulty of obtaining accurate data on the way that the economic impacts of public investments are distributed. In principle, not only must the distributional impact of benefits be ascertained, but also the distributional impact of costs on taxpayers and resource suppliers must be estimated. Some have questioned the practicality of making weighted benefit and cost calculations an integral part of the evaluation process because of the difficulty of accurately estimating these distributional patterns.

Political factors must also be considered in judging the desirability of formally including these calculations in the decision process. Many have argued that when objectives other than economic efficiency become explicitly incorporated into the public expenditure evaluation process, many programs with obsolete purposes will perpetuate themselves by claiming a new income redistribution mission. Similarly, many have questioned the ability of the Congress to publicly decide the optimal set of welfare weights to be incorporated into project evaluation procedures. Indeed, should Congress ever decide on a set of weights, the implications for planning and designing projects are not at all clear. Because the Congress is a transient grouping of individuals and as such is neither rational nor consistent, the weights on which it decides might well oscillate over time. It is not clear that an effective planning process can live with such an oscillating set of "prices."

While the suggestion to incorporate multiple objectives into benefit-cost analysis is as yet unresolved, no one argues that social impacts such as the income distribution effects of a proposed program are irrelevant in deciding whether or not it should be undertaken. All would agree that such information is relevant and that efforts should be made to ascertain these data and make them known in an appropriate form to decision makers.

III. THE PLANNING-PROGRAMING-BUDGETING SYSTEM[27]

In recent years, there has been a major upsurge of interest in applying benefit-cost type analyses to federal government programs. About a decade ago, former Secretary of Defense Robert McNamara introduced a concern for the quantitative evaluation of alternative weapons systems and other policy choices into the Defense Department. He established an office of analysis staffed by a cadre of skilled economists and statisticians and insisted that they present him with hard and quantitative analyses of the "effectiveness" of various alternatives among which choices were to be made. The kind of analysis done by these people came to be called "cost-effectiveness analysis" in that it involved a conscious search for the least costly means of accomplishing explicit national defense objectives.

In August 1965, President Johnson announced that the kind of analysis which had been effective in guiding national defense decisions would be applied to programs in all of the executive agencies. This systematic approach to the analysis of public sector expenditures was incorporated into a Planning-Programing-Budgeting (PPB) System. In President Johnson's words, this system would assist the federal government to:

1. Identify our national goals with precision and on a continuing basis.
2. Choose among those goals the ones that are most urgent.
3. Search for alternative means of reaching those goals most effectively at the least cost.

---

[27] An extensive discussion and critique of both the Planning-Programing-Budgeting System and public expenditure economics is found in U.S. Congress, Joint Economic Committee, Subcommittee on Economy in Government, *The Analysis and Evaluation of Public Expenditures: The PPB System*, 1969.

4. Inform ourselves not merely on next year's costs, but on the second, and third, and subsequent years' costs of our programs.

5. Measure the performance of our programs to insure a dollar's worth of service for each dollar spent.

Stated most simply, the PPB system as applied to public spending decisions requires a rigorous and explicit definition of objectives, a wide consideration of alternatives, a sensitive analysis of benefits and costs of each alternative and, finally, the use of the analysis in the decision process. Without question, this system implies a significant departure from traditional federal government budgetary procedures and a major step toward developing a rational decision-making process.

The Bureau of the Budget, a part of the President's own staff, was given responsibility for implementing the PPB system. As it has evolved, the system contains four main components.

1. *Program structure* has involved the reorganization of the federal budget from an input to an output emphasis. Traditionally, the budget has been organized to demonstrate to the Congress where the money was going in terms of what items were being purchased. This organization made it difficult to relate the costs (inputs) to the outputs which were being produced. Consequently, to serve the objective of program analysis and evaluation, a new structure was devised which would group expenditures by their purpose or objective. In this way the tie between inputs and outputs would be made and the basis for applying economic analysis to the various government programs would be formed.

2. *Program memoranda* are brief documents prepared at the request of the Bureau of the Budget by the federal government agency responsible for a program. Having defined a pertinent policy issue, the Bureau of the Budget requests the agency to review and reconsider the objectives of the program, outline the alternative ways of accomplishing the objective, and estimate the benefits and costs involved in each of these alternatives. In essence, this aspect of the system represents the application of "quick-and-dirty" benefit-cost analysis to the portions of the federal budget on which policy decisions have to be made.

3. *A program and financial plan* represents an attempt to gain a comprehensive picture of the program and activities of an agency. The plan, revised each year, shows the past two years' expenditures for each program administered by an agency, the budget for the current year, and estimates of the expenditures required four years into the future because of commitments and actions already taken. In addition, the plan shows measures of the output of each program, sometimes in dollar terms, but also in physical terms.

4. *Analytic studies* are used to examine in substantial depth major policy issues on which action is likely to be taken. They relate to the program memoranda but are usually of sufficient scope that their preparation requires more time than is available in preparing an annual budget. The objective of these special studies is the accurate evaluation of both social benefits and costs of alternative policies.

The PPB system, then, is the vehicle chosen by the federal government to institute the comprehensive application of economic analysis to public spending alternatives. However, the system has not yet attained its potential. Program memoranda often contain no numbers and serve only as an agency's rationalization of why the *status quo* is optimal. Measures of outputs—let alone benefits—have not yet been derived for many programs. The way in which good economic analysis becomes explicitly relevant in the decision process has not yet been implemented if, indeed, it has been discovered. The ultimate decision maker (in that it controls the purse)—the Congress—often does not see any of the documents that the PPB system generates. Congress, therefore, undertakes major allocation decisions with little or no information on economic impacts. The program structure is still in an experimental stage and often groups together programs with disparate objectives and fails to include those which have similar objectives. Statements of program objectives are often poorly thought out and, in many cases, constructed to convey an impressive picture of hoped-for accomplishments rather than realizable outputs.

While the PPB system embodies a framework and objectives that are essential to an ideal decision-making process, the actual implementation of the system leaves many gains still to be realized. It is helpful to attempt a brief listing of some of the impediments which have hindered progress in this area.

1. In the case of many public programs, the goals or objectives are stated ambiguously or in contradictory ways, or have many dimensions. The responsibility for this lack of clarity lies with both the Congress and the executive branch. One researcher has studied a large number of public programs ranging from atomic energy to manpower training, in an attempt to determine the objectives that the President and Congress had in mind when they proposed and passed the legislation. In over one-half of the programs studied, the objectives of the program "could not be unambiguously identified."[28]

2. As mentioned above, there are many as yet unsolved conceptual problems in the application of economic analysis to public expenditures. While the basic concept of benefit-cost analysis and of the benefit-cost criterion is now widely accepted, significant unresolved issues surround the interest rate for discounting analysis, the use of shadow prices when markets are imperfect or nonexistent, and the consistent handling of objectives other than that of the efficient allocation of resources. Even if these conceptual issues were resolved, the problem of accurately measuring benefits and costs would be a severe one.

3. The PPB system was installed as an adjunct to a budgetary allocation process which, some have claimed, is set in the concrete of tradition. The unyielding character of this process has frustrated many efforts at analysis generated by the PPB system. The tendency to expect overnight changes in this system must be guarded against, especially in the light of the difficult technical and conceptual problems with which the PPB system deals.

4. The implementation of sound and sensitive benefit-cost analysis requires analysts trained in the concepts of economics, the systematic use and analysis of data, and the building of models of "systems." This is, to say the least, scarce talent. Since 1965, over 1000 PPB positions in the federal government have been created which require this talent. That few agency staffs possess

[28] See Harold Hovey, *The Planning-Programing Approach to Government Decision-Making* (New York: Frederick Praeger, 1968), Chap. 9.

III. The Planning-Programing-Budgeting System

the kinds of abilities necessary for competent, on-going analysis is not surprising. Perhaps this factor as much as any has been the primary obstacle to the comprehensive analysis and evaluation of federal spending programs.

5. Many agencies, especially those with programs of marginal economic value, have viewed the PPB system as a threat to their existence or the size of their budget. The response of these agencies has been to lag in implementing sound analysis of their activities. Given the range of conceptual difficulties plaguing quantitative benefit-cost analysis, an agency that feels threatened can easily cite the difficulties of analysis in rationalizing the failure to undertake it. Indeed, in some agencies it appears that as much creative thought has gone into devising ways to avoid the sound economic analysis of policies and programs as into implementing such analysis.

6. The role of Congress in encouraging or insisting on the competent analysis of programs has been a mixed bag. As we have seen, the appropriation process established by the Congress is not conducive to the careful consideration of alternatives or to the meaningful discussion of objectives or priorities. Moreover, many Congressmen and Senators with significant power fear that careful benefit-cost analysis will infringe on their personal ability to control segments of the federal budget. They recognize well that nothing erodes vested power like widely disseminated information and objective analysis. Finally, neither individual Congressmen nor the Congress itself has sufficient staff with the training necessary to interpret, digest, or apply alternative assumptions to analyses produced by the executive agencies and bureaus. For these reasons, Congress, at best, has been apprehensive about and indifferent to the PPB system and, at worst, openly antagonistic both to policy analysis and to policy analysts. Perhaps the nadir of the Congressional response was the attempt by Congressman Mendel Rivers, the Chairman of the House Armed Services Committee, to eliminate through legislation the position and office of the Assistant Secretary of Defense for Systems Analysis. This office, created by former Defense Secretary McNamara, has responsibility for applying economic analysis to expenditure proposals in that agency—the largest in the federal government.

7. A successful PPB system which brings economic analysis to bear in the decision process would threaten the ability of private interest groups to influence public spending favorable to themselves. It would be substantially more difficult for these groups to sustain support for the program which furnished them a subsidy if sound analysis showed the prospective costs of the program to exceed its anticipated benefits. These private interest groups, consequently, have furnished significant opposition to the development of sound analytical practices in evaluating certain public undertakings. As implied above, they have not been without their allies in either the executive agencies or the Congress.

An example of the efforts of these groups relates to the size of the interest rate used for discounting analysis. In recent years, the interest rate used in evaluating water development projects has been an inappropriately low 3 percent. In 1968 the President urged that the rate be raised to about 4½ percent.[29] This proposal was met by substantial opposition from those vested interest groups subsidized by federal water resource development (land owners wanting cheap water for irrigation, real estate developers, people living in flood plains, businesses which ship goods by waterway, barge lines, and so on).[30] Similarly, the previously cited Congressman's attempt to abolish the economic evaluation office in the Department of Defense was not without the strong support of the "military-minded" in the Pentagon and defense contractors producing weapons and other military hardware.

IV. PUBLIC OUTPUTS AND THE PRICING SYSTEM

Like the outputs of private businesses, public outputs are of value to people. In fact, in discussing the procedures for estimating the benefits of public programs, we emphasized that the "willingness of people to pay" for these outputs is the correct definition of their value. A natural question then is: "If people are willing to pay to obtain these outputs, why shouldn't the government permit them to; why should the cost of providing them be paid by the general

[29] The higher rate was justified by the President in that it was related to the current yield on government bonds.
[30] Their efforts in this case were unsuccessful—one of their few failures.

taxpayer?" While there are good reasons why the pricing system cannot serve to allocate some of these outputs among people, the question is a legitimate one. Indeed, there is reason to believe that the sale of certain public outputs would be both more equitable and more efficient than the common practice of giving them away.

As we have seen, the private market system incorporates the ethic that people should get only what they pay for. If this value judgment is applicable for privately produced goods, why is it not acceptable also for the outputs of public programs? As a matter of fact, failure to follow the same rule in both sectors smacks of a kind of injustice. If students at private colleges are required to pay tuition for their privately produced education, why should the users of public colleges not be required to pay for their education?

Although the private sector "you-get-what-you-pay-for" ethic does carry some weight, there are other value judgments which often effectively counter it—even for public outputs which are subject to the exclusion principle. In the case of some public outputs, society has found it desirable to apply the principle of "available-to-all-whether-or-not-they-can-afford-it" instead of the private sector ethic. For example, in some places, school lunches are supplied free to all children. Similarly, elementary and secondary education, the use of city parks and streets, flood control measures, and so on are provided without charge. In choosing this free-to-all distribution ethic for some goods, society has rejected the private sector ethic, and has substituted the judgment that these goods and services should be provided to all people as a *right* and not withheld from them if they are unable (or unwilling) to pay for them.

In addition to the "you-get-what-you-pay-for" equity principle, there is a second basis for arguing that public outputs should be sold and not given away—economic efficiency. Stated most baldly, giving public outputs away will result either in *overproduction* or in *shortage* (which sometimes shows up as congestion) or both. In either of these cases, there will be a misallocation of resources or economic waste.

A few examples should make this clear. Consider a no-charge municipal swimming pool on a hot Sunday afternoon. To observe the number of bodies crowded into a few square feet, one would be led to believe that there was an extreme shortage of swimming facilities. And indeed there is if one feels that Sunday afternoon swimming should be provided at the same price as air for breathing—*zero*. In fact, there would be a shortage of all goods from steaks to medical care to automobiles if they were sold at a zero price. To give a good away is to stimulate use of it by all people from those who value it highly to those who will choose to use it *only* if there is no charge. If a good is given away, people will continue to demand it as long as its value to them is anything above zero. Consequently, when a person who values the pool only a little is allowed to swim for free on a hot Sunday afternoon, the marginal benefit of the pool to him may well be less than the marginal cost in the form of decreased enjoyment by others due to the addition of his body. When marginal cost exceeds marginal benefit, resources are being allocated inefficiently. The *shortage* or *congestion* which is often associated with goods or services provided without charge is evidence of this inefficiency.

As another example of the inefficiency which results when an output is underpriced, consider the U.S. postal system. Currently, the postal rates charged for handling some kinds of mail are kept substantially below marginal cost. Indeed, the Post Office runs at a deficit of nearly $1 billion per year. Because of the low rates, especially on advertising or "junk mail," companies are encouraged to use the mails for their advertising campaigns and the Post Office Department is required to supplement its delivery and sorting staffs and to devote additional resources to transporting the mail. To the extent that the cost (to the Post Office and, hence, to society) of this additional mail service exceeds the value of the service, more output is being produced than is economical. The waste of social resources implied by this *overproduction* is due to the underpricing of mail service.

Similarly, one finds exceedingly strong pressures for the overproduction of public works projects. If, for example, there is a chance that the federal government will construct a waterway from the Gulf of Mexico to Fort Worth, Texas, and provide it free of charge to the area, there will be a great volume of activity (most of it political) to have that waterway constructed whether or not its total costs exceed its total benefits. Again, the tendency is toward overproduction due to underpricing.

If, then, the failure to charge for public outputs leads to shortage, congestion, overproduction, and a misallocation of resources, why are so few "user fees" or prices imposed by governments? Although part of the answer rests with the equity principle of "available-to-all-whether-or-not-they-can-afford-it," another reason relates to the technical characteristics of the goods produced by governments. As we discussed in Chapters 2 and 3, certain of these goods, like national defense, are not subject to the exclusion principle. They are public goods. Because no one can be excluded from enjoying these goods once they are produced, there is no basis for charging for them other than through general tax revenues. Much the same is true for outputs which have large externalities or spillovers, like elementary education or the administration of a legal system. Again, one is hard pressed to charge for that portion of the benefit for which there is no direct beneficiary. Finally, the very high "transaction" costs involved in selling some outputs also constrain use of the pricing mechanism. To charge for municipal water supply requires a costly meter to be installed in every house or apartment, people to read the meters regularly, people and machines and the postal system to bill customers, and so on. While some cities use this mechanism to sell water, others find it too expensive. Because of high transaction costs, for example, no cities charge motorists for the miles of city streets which they use in a year.[31]

Although there are impediments to charging for governmentally produced goods and services, the potential for increasing the use of the pricing system is great. In recent years, there has been discussion of and serious consideration given to increasing the use of beneficiary charges or user fees on a number of our public programs. Among them one finds proposals for increasing the fees on publicly provided recreation facilities, irrigation water, grazing privileges, mineral claims, highways, airport facilities and, particularly, the services of institutions of higher education. It has been proposed that charges be placed on those who pollute streams or the air or who ruin the landscape. Such charges have

[31] The rule that should guide the public sector in cases in which the equity considerations are not overriding is one which we have encountered before. Prices should be charged on public outputs in each case in which the costs of pricing are less than the benefits.

substantial economic rationale. Similarly, it is being increasingly suggested that the programs that have been provided to regions or communities free of charge, such as sewage facilities, flood control facilities, and harbors, be financed through charges placed on beneficiary groups. These proposals are usually referred to as beneficiary cost-sharing arrangements. In general, it appears that there are a large number of areas in which federal government policy could be improved by increased use of the pricing, user charge, or beneficiary cost-sharing mechanism.

V. SUMMARY AND CONCLUSIONS

This chapter has examined a number of issues pertinent to the expenditure side of the budget. We have analyzed the process by which public spending decisions are made. We took special note of the bargaining mechanism which is incorporated into the political system. This mechanism, if operating effectively, takes into account the costs and gains of a wide range of interests and functions as an "invisible hand" in public decision making. However, because this process is an imperfect one, it is necessary that economic analysis be applied to public spending proposals so that the social costs and benefits of each alternative can be seen by decision makers.

The application of economic analysis to public expenditures— called benefit-cost or cost-effectiveness analysis—was described in some detail. We discussed both the benefit-cost criterion— maximum present value of net benefits—and some conceptual and measurement problems encountered in applying this kind of analysis to public spending decisions. A recent attempt to develop a rational and systematic decision process in the federal government was described and the difficulties which the implementation of the PPB system has encountered were outlined.

Finally, the reasons for and against using the pricing system to distribute public outputs were explored. While there are a number of factors which make the use of "user fees" undesirable, impossible, or uneconomic, we judged that there is substantial room for the increased use of this mechanism. Appropriate application of beneficiary charges would contribute to the efficiency of government expenditure policy.

9

The Public Debt—Its Burden and Impact

In Part Four, we have examined the public budget. Although we have discussed the economics of both government revenues and expenditures, our treatment of the budget is not yet complete. Because public expenditures have, on balance, exceeded public revenues over the course of U.S. history, a sizeable national debt has accumulated. The existence of this indebtedness has generated heated debate and has become a political issue. In this chapter we shall analyze the economics of the public debt.

I. SOME FACTS ABOUT THE NATIONAL DEBT

On January 1, 1970, the debt of the federal government totaled about $360 billion. In the most basic sense, this public debt is the same as an individual, family, or business debt. It represents a flow of spending which has exceeded a flow of income over a period of time. This short-fall of income—a deficit—can exist only if the debtor borrows money from someone who has experienced an excess of income over spending—a surplus.[1] That is, budget deficits generate borrowing. In turn, the act of borrowing

---

[1] In this discussion it is assumed that the liquidation of assets is not used to cover a deficit. In the real world, individuals and institutions often cover a temporary deficit by selling some assets—some real estate or some stocks or bonds. The national government, because it has the constitutional authority to print money, could cover a deficit by creating additional money.

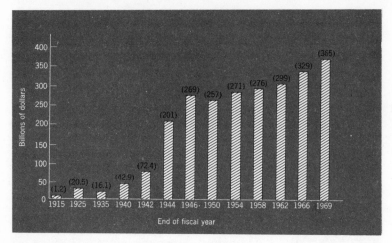

Figure 9-1

creates debt. When a government borrows, the debt is a public debt.

When borrowing occurs, a *debt instrument* is created. This is a legal paper giving evidence that a lender-borrower relationship exists between two parties. Debt instruments come in various forms and are known by various names—I.O.U.s, notes, and bonds are some of the most common. Nearly all debt instruments specify certain information, including the name of the borrower, the amount of the loan, the price of the loan (the interest rate), and the date by which the loan is to be repaid. The instrument is held by the lender, and it is his evidence of a claim on the borrower. When the U.S. government borrows, the debt instrument which is created is known as a government bond.[2] Consequently, on January 1, 1970, there were about $360 billion worth of U.S. government securities outstanding.

The vast bulk of the federal debt has been accumulated in the last 30 years. Indeed, the debt today is approximately nine times the size of the national debt in 1939. Figure 9-1 shows the pattern of growth in the debt since early in this century. As can be seen there, the large bulk of the debt was accumulated during World

[2] In addition to bonds, which are usually issued for long-term borrowings, there are government bills and notes, which are short-term securities.

War II. In the five years of the war, over $200 billion was borrowed by the federal government. While the debt has grown since 1946, most of the postwar increase is attributable to the Korean and Vietnam Wars and the intermittent periods of excessive unemployment which kept the national income and, consequently, tax revenues from being as high as they otherwise would have been.

The low postwar growth of the federal debt is in contrast to the growth of both private debt—that owed by individuals and businesses—and state and local government debt. In 1947, for example, the private debt and national debt were about equal in volume. Today the volume of private debt exceeds that of U.S. government debt by three times. Like private debt, the growth of state and local government debt has been very rapid since the late 1940s.

While the absolute size of the debt is very large and growing, its size relative to the nation's income or the GNP has been falling steadily since 1946. This is shown in the top chart of Figure 9-2. From the high ratio of debt to GNP of about 130 percent which

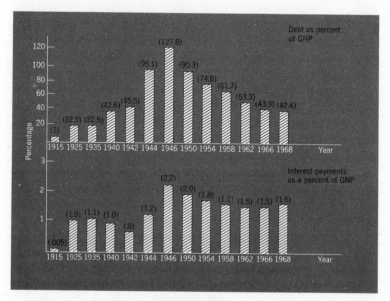

Figure 9-2

was experienced in 1946, the ratio has fallen to about 40 percent today. The high ratio of 1946 is clearly attributable to the decision to finance much of the cost of World War II through borrowing. It should also be noted that the size of the debt relative to the population has fallen since World War II. While in 1946 the debt amounted to $1899 for every living American, today each American's share is $1816.

Although the debt as a proportion of GNP has been steadily falling since 1946, the level of interest payments by the government to bondholders has been relatively constant, fluctuating between 1.5 and 2.0 percent of GNP. This is shown in the bottom chart of Figure 9-2. This interest-payment-to-GNP-ratio has failed to fall because of the rising trend of interest rates in the United States. As old low interest rate bonds have become due, the government has replaced them by selling new bonds carrying higher interest rates.

II. SOME ASSERTIONS ABOUT THE NATIONAL DEBT

During the past 20 years, the existence and size of the national debt have been a controversial public policy issue. Many claims have been made concerning the evils or dangers of the debt; most of them without basis. In this section, we shall consider a few of these assertions and evaluate their legitimacy.

A. "A Public Debt as Large as that of the United States Can Lead a Nation to Bankruptcy"

This common assertion is based on the belief that public debts have the same implications for the people who owe them as do private debts. Just as an individual or business with excessive indebtedness can be declared insolvent and drawn into bankruptcy, so, too, this proposition implies, can a national government. Three comments are pertinent to this conjecture.

First, because of the people who have loaned the U.S. government money, the U.S. public debt is not subject to the same kind of forces as a private debt. By definition, the lender involved in nearly all private debts is a person or an institution which is legally different than the debtor; that is, there is a lender who can make a legal claim on the debtor's assets when the time for payment of the debt is at hand. Such a debt is an *external* debt; the lender is external to the borrower.

The national debt, however, is an *internal* debt because the people who owe the debt (U.S. citizens) are the same people as those to whom the debt is owed. This is because over 95 percent of the outstanding U.S. government bonds are held either by U.S. citizens or by banks and other institutions which are themselves owned by U.S. citizens. That is to say, U.S. citizens have loaned their government over 95 percent of the dollars which it owes. This pattern of debt ownership is shown in Table 9-1. Because of

Table 9-1.   Pattern of U.S. National Debt Ownership, October 1968

Class of Debt Holders	Percent of Total Debt Outstanding
U.S. government accounts	22.0
Commercial banks	18.1
Federal Reserve banks	14.9
Individuals	21.2
Insurance companies	2.2
Mutual savings banks	1.0
Corporations	4.0
State and local governments	7.5
Foreign	3.8
Other	5.2
	100.0

Source. U.S. Treasury, *Treasury Bulletin,* December, 1968.

this pattern of ownership, the people who would demand repayment of the debt are the very ones who would be called on to do the repaying. In a very real sense, we owe the debt to ourselves in much the same way as do the members of a country club who have loaned the club some money to finance, say, a new swimming pool. If a debt is internally held, the notion that it can lead to bankruptcy is unfounded.

Second, it should be noted that the national debt of the United States relative to its GNP is not particularly large in comparison to the debt-GNP ratio of many other major nations. The United Kingdom, for example, has a national debt which is about 120 percent of its GNP. Moreover, a larger proportion of the British national debt is externally held. Even in this case, there is no danger of national bankruptcy resulting from a large public debt.

Finally, it should be recognized that the real causes of national bankruptcy are much more basic and deep-seated than state indebtedness. Constitutional crises are stimulated by a fundamental lack of confidence in the government, such as might be caused by deep and prolonged economic depression or unremedied social injustice. They are not generated by the existence of a public debt—especially not in a nation whose government is constitutionally granted the power to raise revenue through taxation.

B. *"The National Debt and Deficit Spending Are Inflationary"*

For some typically unexplained reason, it is often claimed that the public debt and deficit spending cause prices to rise. While this may be a correct assertion under certain conditions, it does not hold as a general proposition. This can be shown by reference to both reason and the facts.

Among those who study the economy, it is generally accepted that the primary cause of rising prices is an imbalance between the total demand for goods and services and the nation's ability to supply the amount demanded. When consumers, businessmen, and governments wish to buy more than the economy can supply, businesses are found operating at capacity, their inventories are being exhausted, and the backlog of orders is growing. This pressure on supply will drive prices up—the essence of inflation.

Clearly, government decisions can either aggravate or ease a situation in which there is too much aggregate demand and rising prices. For example, assume that in a fully employed economy with rising prices, the government spends an additional $1 million which it finances by borrowing $1 million (hence, creating a $1 million deficit). The entire volume of this additional spending gets added to aggregate demand. On the other hand, only part of the borrowing leads to a reduction of aggregate demand. While part of this borrowing will come out of what people would otherwise be spending, part of it will come out of savings. On balance, aggregate demand will be reduced by less than the amount which is borrowed. Consequently, the *net* effect of a deficit is to add to aggregate demand and, therefore, to feed the inflationary fire. When there is no idle supply capacity, therefore, deficit spending —adding to the national debt—can be inflationary.

On the other hand, if the economy were in recession, deficit spending would create some necessary aggregate demand and would contribute to a reduction in unemployment. The net addition to aggregate demand caused by the borrowing-spending decision would have beneficial effects. Moreover, because there is insufficient rather than excess aggregate demand in this situation, there would be no increase in prices due to the deficit.

Economic logic, then, argues that the state of the economy makes all the difference in appraising the effect of deficit spending on the price level. If there is full employment, deficit spending may be inflationary; if there is slack in the economy, deficit financing is both desirable and noninflationary.

This logic is reinforced by a cursory look at the statistics which relate deficit spending to changes in the price level. One recent comparison associated several statistical definitions of federal deficits with several measures of price increases for the years 1949–1967. This study concluded that the influence of deficits on changes in the price level was nonexistent. In fact, the author argued that coin-flipping would do as well in predicting price increases as would the presence or absence of a deficit. While the test used was a crude one, it does give some indication of the lack of a relationship between these variables.[3]

C. *"We Are Passing the Burden of our Spending onto Future Generations"*

This statement, like the previous two, has been uttered repeatedly by those who oppose deficit spending and fear the national debt. Its weakness stems from a failure to distinguish financial transfers from real economic effects. The distinction between these concepts becomes clear when the massive government borrowing to finance World War II is analyzed. By selling bonds to people living during that war, the government was able to finance its spending for munitions, armaments, and military manpower. The national debt created by this borrowing exists yet today and is an outstanding obligation of the current government and the current body of taxpayers. Even though this national financial obligation is still

[3] D. J. Edwards, "The Association of Federal Deficits, GNP Growth, and Money Growth with Interest-Rate and Prices Changes," *Journal of Political Economy*, **77**, March-April 1969, pp. 286-290.

outstanding, it must be emphasized that the *real cost* of fighting World War II consisted of the resources withdrawn from the economy at that time to support the effort. This cost includes the luxuries, and sometimes necessities, done without during those years, and the lives lost. The drastic reduction in the nation's capital stock and real wealth during the war also represents costs imposed on that generation. These real economic costs were borne primarily by the people living then, and not by today's generation.

But what about the debt which today's generation has inherited? Will it not impose a burden on us to repay that debt? Because it is an internal debt, today's generation has inherited both the obligation to pay it (as citizens) and the right to receive the payment (as bondholders). While some part of today's generation has inherited a debt (taxpayers), another part of today's generation has inherited bonds. Indeed, these two groups include many of the same people. Because of the "we owe it to ourselves" character of an internal debt, these two effects cancel each other and today's generation inherits no *net* burden because of the debt. Similarly, deficit spending today imposes no real economic burden on future generations.[4]

III. SOME BENEFITS AND COSTS OF THE NATIONAL DEBT

The lack of basis for some assertions concerning the national debt should not be taken to imply that its existence has no real social

---

[4] It should be noted, however, that while generally accepted, this point is not conceded by all observers. Some economists point out that under certain circumstances, the generation which originally sacrificed consumption in order to buy the bonds may regain that consumption later by selling the bonds to a new generation. If the new generation decides to pay off the debt, people in that generation will have to forego some consumption and, hence, bear a part of the burden. In that way, some of the burden may be shifted to future generations. For a more detailed statement of this position, see W. G. Bowen, R. G. Davis, and D. H. Kopf, "The Public Debt: A Burden on Future Generations," *American Economic Review*, September 1960; pp. 701-6. See also, J. M. Buchanan, *Public Principles of Public Debt* (Homewood, Ill.: Richard D. Irwin, Inc., 1958), who argues that, in all likelihood, the full burden of the debt *is* shifted to future generations.

gains or costs. In this section, a few of these real economic impacts will be discussed briefly.

A. *Some Benefits of the National Debt*

Without question, a most important benefit of the existence of the national debt is that it provides a flexible means of accommodating budget deficits and surpluses. As can be seen from a study of macroeconomics,[5] the flexible use of federal revenues and expenditures (and the deficit or surplus relationship between them) is essential to the maintenance of a stable and fully employed economy.

Because the level of GNP is related both to public spending and to taxes through their effect on the level of aggregate demand, these two budgetary variables become policy instruments which can be altered so as to keep GNP high enough to maintain full employment and low enough to avoid inflationary pressures. As the 1968 Report of the President's Council of Economic Advisers stated:

The economy's aggregate demand is the total of spending for final output by all groups—consumers, business, government, and foreign buyers. When aggregate demand matches supply capability, resources are fully utilized and production equals the economy's potential. If aggregate demand should fall short of supply capability, part of the output that the economy is capable of turning out would not be produced, and some resources would be wasted in idleness. On the other hand, excessive demand—too much spending in relation to potential output—would generate inflationary pressures on prices and costs. The basic task of [taxing and spending] . . . policies is to help ensure a match between demand and productive potential.[6]

For example, when the economy is overheated, as it was during 1969, consumers, businesses, and governments desire to buy more goods and services than the economy is able to produce. Because of excessive aggregate demand, prices tend to rise and inflation is a major problem. Both federal taxes and expenditures can be used to correct this situation. If public spending is cut

[5] See Arnold Collery, *National Income and Employment Analysis,* in this series.
[6] U.S. Government, *Economic Report of the President,* 1968, pp. 61-62.

back, aggregate demand is reduced from what it would otherwise be and inflationary pressures are reduced. If taxes are increased, households and business have less to spend than they would otherwise and, similarly, aggregate demand and inflationary pressures are reduced. In an overheated economy, then, the need for reduced public expenditures and increased taxes imply the desirability of a budget surplus—a reduction of the debt.[7] Conversely, when the economy is operating at less than full employment, increased government spending and reduced taxes should be the marching orders, implying a deficit in the public budget and an increase in the public debt.

The point, then, is clear: the existence of a public debt provides a sponge to absorb funds when a budgetary surplus is needed and to release funds when a deficit is called for. It enables a flexible fiscal policy composed of planned surpluses in an overheated economy and planned deficits to stimulate an economy with unemployed resources.

A second benefit of the debt relates to the financial system of the United States. During any period of time, a large number of individuals, businesses, governments, and other institutions take in more income than they spend. That is to say, they save. For each of the savers, a relevant question is: "What shall I do with my savings, other than place them in a stocking?" Clearly there are a number of alternatives—among them are checking accounts, savings accounts, stocks, corporation bonds, state and local bonds, personal loans, life insurance, and U.S. government bonds. Of all of these instruments to absorb savings, U.S. government bonds are the safest and entail little if any risk of default. In fact, many of the other instruments appear so safe and riskless because they are simply an indirect way of buying these bonds. For example, money placed in savings accounts appears so safe largely because banks use a large proportion of their deposits to buy U.S. government bonds. Savings accounts, then, are to a significant extent "backed" by the debt of the U.S. government and its promise to

[7] It should be noted that the Nixon Administration, confronting the inflationary situation of early 1969, advocated (1) reduced Federal spending, (2) continuance of the surtax on personal and corporate incomes, and (3) a shift from the FY 1969 budget deficit of about $25 billion to a FY 1970 budget surplus of $5+ billion.

pay when bonds become due. Similarly, many large government trust funds, such as the social security trust fund, are stable and of low risk because of their substantial holdings of Federal government securities. It would not be stretching the case to call the national debt the "backbone" of the U.S. financial system. If the national debt were erased, the nation would be deprived of the safest and most risk-free block of credit instruments that it has.

B. *Some Costs of the National Debt*

While the existence of a sizeable national debt has social benefits, it also imposes certain constraints and social costs. One of the most significant of these is attributable to the interest that must be paid on all bonds which become due. As we have seen, each year's federal budget includes a major item for these interest payments. For example, it is estimated that nearly $16 billion dollars will be required in FY 1970 to cover interest payments on the national debt. This is about 9 percent of the total federal budget—a sizeable slice. Because of this unavoidable (as long as there is a debt) expenditure, the federal budget and, therefore, taxes are higher that they would otherwise be.

The annual interest charge has economic effects which operate through both the revenue and the expenditure sides of the budget. As mentioned in Chapter 7, the imposition of taxes on the society is likely to entail real costs, real losses of productivity. This economic impact results from both the distortions in the allocation of resources caused by certain kinds of taxes and the effect of taxes on incentives and abilities.

In our discussion of excise taxes, for example, we saw that the output of a taxed commodity was restricted below the socially optimal level. At the after-tax equilibrium level of output, marginal social gain exceeds marginal cost. We argued that this distorted equilibrium indicates a misallocation of national resources and economic inefficiency. To the extent that these kinds of taxes are increased to cover interest payments on the national debt, misallocation of resources and economic waste are greater than they would otherwise be. This is a social cost attributable to the existence of the public debt.

Similarly, social costs may be generated if the imposition of taxes to cover interest payments adversely affects the willingness (or incentive) of people to work, save, and invest. While the effect of taxes on incentives may work in either direction, the distinct possibility that taxes to cover interest payments on the debt may entail a real loss of output should not be ignored.

The national debt and its required interest payments may also impose costs on the society through the expenditure side of the budget. Because of the large and unavoidable debt interest item in the budget, the society may be constrained in the use of tax revenues to accomplish desirable and productive social objectives. If, as many argue, resistance to increased federal spending rises with the size of the budget, the unavoidable $16 billion interest payment item tends to restrain increases in federal expenditures for other objectives. While some would claim that anything which restricted the size of the federal budget was a benefit, those holding an economic point of view would not. If productive and worthwhile alternatives in the public sector have to be foregone because of the constraining effect of the interest payment item, a real social cost is imposed on the society. Arbitrary limitations on the size of the budget together with the unavoidable expense of interest payments may mean that net benefits from worthwhile public expenditures are not realized by the society.

A second major concern of the national debt relates to its equity impact—its effect on the nation's income distribution. If one is worried about how society's income is distributed, the pattern of collection and disbursement of the several billion dollars of annual interest payments may be cause for concern. If the distribution of taxes collected from people of various income and social levels was identical to the distribution of interest payments, there would be no problem. The existence of the debt and interest payments would have no net effect on the distribution of society's after-tax income.

In fact, it appears that the taxes collected and interest payments made do not neutralize each other in this way. The federal tax system, we have seen, collects the bulk of its revenue from people in the middle and upper-middle income ranges.[8] Interest payments are distributed among the income classes in proportion to the dis-

8 See Table 6-2.

tribution of U.S. government bonds. Bond holdings appear to be somewhat more concentrated among the very highest income people than are federal tax revenues.[9] On balance, then, it is likely that interest payments on the public debt transfers income from lower to higher income people. The composite taxation-expenditure effect tends to make the income distribution more unequal than it otherwise would be.

Clearly, whether one classifies this equity effect of the national debt as a cost or a benefit is a value judgment. We have classified it as a cost on the assumption that a more equal distribution of income is preferred by society to one that is less equal.

There is one final cost impact that is often attributed to deficit spending and the national debt. For a number of reasons, none of which appears to be entirely convincing, some people have argued that when the government borrows to finance its spending, *private* investment spending is discouraged.

One reason given for this effect pertains to the impact of government borrowing on interest rates. It has been argued, that, if there is full employment and if the government finances its spending by selling bonds, interest rates will tend to be bid up and some funds will be diverted from private investment. To the extent that this is so, the private capital stock will fail to grow as fast as it otherwise would have. If this occurs, a real cost must be tallied up against the public debt.

Another effect which is alleged to discourage private investment is a purely psychological phenomenon. It is asserted that the very existence of the public debt has an adverse effect on the expectations of businessmen who do not clearly perceive its significance (or lack of significance). Again, to the extent that real business investment is curtailed because of this phenomenon, a social cost must be attributed to the existence of the national debt. It should be emphasized, however, that conjectures on the relationship between the debt and the level of private investment spending are, at best, highly speculative. They are neither proven nor disproven by evidence.

---

[9] Table 6-6, for example, suggests that families with incomes in excess of $10,000 per year receive more in federal interest payments than they receive from all federal housing, education, social security, agriculture, and health programs *combined.*

IV. SUMMARY AND CONCLUSIONS

This chapter has connected the two sides of the federal budget. If the two sides fail to be equal, there is either a budgetary surplus or a deficit. The national debt is obtained by adding together all of the budget deficits and subtracting from this number all of the surpluses. At the beginning of 1970, the size of the debt was about $360 billion.

Over 50 percent of the debt was accumulated during World War II. Since that time, it has grown slowly. Indeed, the burden of the debt as measured by the nation's ability to pay the interest and to repay the debt has fallen substantially since 1946.

Discussions of the national debt have often been clouded by misleading assertions about dangers created by its existence. These dangers relate to the alleged influence of the debt on inflation, national bankruptcy, and the immorality of passing the burden of one generation's spending on to a later generation. In evaluating these allegations, we found little of substance in them. In large part, they are misleading because they fail to recognize that the U.S. national debt is internally held; that U.S. citizens, in a very real sense, owe the debt to themselves.

While these allegations failed to assist us in evaluating the impact of the national debt, its existence does entail a number of real costs and benefits. On the advantage or benefit side, we saw that the national debt enables a flexible and stabilizing fiscal policy and provides a large block of low-risk and negotiable instruments which serve as the backbone of the financial system. The disadvantages of the debt relate to the real costs of higher taxes and a higher budget to cover interest payments, its adverse effect in redistributing income from lower to higher income people, and the possible harmful effect of public deficits on the level of private investment.

PART FIVE

10

Some Current Issues in Public Economics

A fundamental argument of this volume is that the formation of sound public policy requires the sensitive evaluation of alternatives, that is, the application of policy analysis. Consequently, as policy makers focus on one issue today and on another tomorrow, so, too, must the practitioners of public sector economics. In this final chapter, we shall take a brief look at some of the economic considerations that surround three prominent policy issues. Although each of the issues is complex, our discussions will be brief and introductory; we shall not attempt to resolve any one of them. The policy problems which we shall discuss are (1) the negative income tax proposal, (2) the matter of "tax expenditures" and tax credits, and (3) the problem of the military budget and national priorities.

I. NEGATIVE INCOME TAXATION

During the last decade, the nation's attention has been drawn to the problem of poverty and the social conditions which accompany it. This national concern has stimulated a search for appropriate public policies with which to deal with the problem. One simple and direct proposal developed in this search is the negative income tax. Among other reasons, this proposal has been supported by both liberals and conservatives because of its simplicity and directness. Basically, this proposal calls for the extension of the personal income tax structure[1] into the low income and poverty classes, but with the government making payments to individuals in these classes rather than collecting revenues. Therefore, the negative income tax is a means of guaranteeing a minimum level of income to everybody, irrespective of how much income is earned by working.

A. *Poverty and the War Against It*[2]

Nearly all Americans place the problem of poverty high among the list of the nation's problems. This judgment is given basis in the statistics and other evidence on low incomes, inadequate living conditions and, indeed, hunger in the United States. A brief recital of some of these facts is worthwhile.

- While median family income in the United States was nearly $8000 in 1967, about 26 million people lived below the poverty level.[3]
- Nearly one-third of all nonwhite families have incomes below the poverty cutoff level.
- While the unemployment rate for the nation was about 3.5 percent in 1968, the rate of unemployment in the nation's ghetto areas was well over 10 percent; for Negro teenagers, it was about 25 percent.
- Poor people pay significantly higher prices for the goods and services which they purchase than do middle and high income people.
- The social characteristics related to poverty are high incidence of malnutrition and hunger, staggering school dropout rates, discrimination in housing and employment, inferior housing and sanitary conditions, and families without a male head.

In the face of these conditions, our society has responded with a number of programs designed to supplement family income. In

[1] There are a number of proposals that are not related to the income tax structure but that accomplish the same objective as the negative income tax. One of these is the "Guaranteed Annual Income." Another is President Nixon's "Family Assistance Plan," announced in August 1969. We shall briefly discuss this latter plan as an alternative to the negative income tax.
[2] See also Alan Batchelder, *The Economics of Poverty*, in this series.
[3] The poverty line is drawn at about $3550 per year for a non-farm family of four.

fact, in fiscal year 1969, nearly $60 billion was spent by the federal government on programs designed to provide assistance to people in various circumstances. These range from unemployment insurance programs to social security programs to old age assistance to the food stamp program. The breakdown of expenditures on these programs is shown in Table 10-1.

A number of things should be noted about these programs. First, each of them is "categorical" in that a family has to display certain characteristics in order to qualify for the program. For example, only former members of the armed forces can qualify for the veterans' benefit programs and only those without sight can qualify for aid to the blind. Consequently, a large number of poor families fail to qualify for assistance from these sources. Second, while each of these programs has the maintenance of people's income as one of their primary objectives, many of them provide a large proportion of their benefits to people with incomes in excess of the poverty line. For example, according to Table 10-1, only 36 percent of Medicare benefits buys medical services for the poor. Indeed, a 1967 study noted that only slightly more than 50 percent of *all* transfer payments were received by families who would have been below the poverty line without them.[4] The effectiveness of these programs in attacking poverty is reduced to the extent that they are spread over the general population, rather than being concentrated among the poor. However, while these income transfer programs are categorical and, in some cases, not aimed at poor families, they have provided major assistance to low income people. It has recently been estimated that these programs reduce the number of people below the poverty line by about 30 percent; that without these programs, about 12 to 15 million people now classified as non-poor would be reduced to the poverty group.[5]

Finally, it must be emphasized that, although this system of assistance is a sizable one, it does not come close to eliminating poverty. The concept of the "poverty gap" is helpful in understanding the basis of this statement. The poverty gap is defined as the volume of money necessary to provide all people now living

[4] Christopher Green, *Negative Taxes and the Poverty Problem* (Washington: The Brookings Institution, 1967), p. 20.
[5] *Ibid.*, pp. 16-20.

Table 10-1. Federal Transfer and Income Supplement Programs, FY 1969

All Programs	Total Outlays (Millions of Dollars)	Percent of Beneficiaries with Income less than $3000
	$58,679	N.A.
Aid to families with dependent children	3,206	100
Unemployment insurance		
Federal-state unemployment compensation	2,300	20
Federal employees and ex-servicemen	111	10
Railroad	52	N.A.
Disability programs		
Workmen's compensation	1,686	N.A.
Federal employees	57	15
Veterans' compensation	2,611	24
Railroad	77	N.A.
Social Security	2,691	39
Aid to the blind	92	100
Aid to the permanently and totally disabled	726	100
Assistance to those 65 years and over		
Social security retirement and survivors' benefits	24,681	31
Old-age assistance	1,833	100
Military retirement	2,265	N.A.
Civil service retirement	2,364	N.A.
Railroad retirement	1,542	34
Veterans' pensions	2,127	80
General assistance	32	100
Assistance-in-kind	10,226	N.A.
Food programs	665	—
Food stamps	273	100
Child nutrition	128	100
Special supplementary package	9	100
Other direct distribution	255	100
Housing programs	484	—
Public housing	456	57
Rent supplements	28	67

All Programs	Total Outlays (Millions of Dollars)	Percent of Beneficiaries with Income less than $3000
Health Service programs	9,077	—
Medicare	6,222	36
Medicaid	2,384	75
Maternity and infant care	193	70
Public Health Service Medical programs		
Indians, seamen, etc.	175	55
Neighborhood health centers	103	75

Source. Economic Report of the President, 1968, pp. 164 and 167.

below the poverty line sufficient income to lift them above the line. If, for example, the poverty line were at $3000 and there was only one family below the line and that family earned $1000 of income, the poverty gap would be $2000; if there were two families, one with $1000 and one with $1500 of income, the poverty gap would be $3500. It has been estimated that, without the system of transfer programs existing in 1961, the poverty gap would have been about $18 billion in that year. However, because of these programs, the poverty gap was reduced by over $10 billion, to about $7.5 billion.[6] While the set of income assistance programs existing in 1961 closed about three-fifths of the poverty gap, nearly 9 million families were left living in poverty.[7]

B. *Negative Income Tax Proposals*

Proposals for a negative income tax have at least two objectives. Without question, their primary aim is to reduce (or eliminate) the poverty gap. In addition, it is anticipated that a number of the undesirable features of the existing income support system

[6] *Ibid.*

[7] A more recent report, issued by the Bureau of the Census in early 1970, estimated that in 1968 it would have taken about $10 billion to close the poverty gap. That report used a revised poverty threshhold level in which changes in the cost of living were included in the definition of the poverty line.

could be eliminated by means of a negative income tax plan.[8] For example, because the negative income tax is comprehensive and not categorical, it would assist all poor people and not just those meeting certain, often arbitrary, requirements. It guarantees a minimum of income to each individual as a matter of "right."

Another characteristic of existing welfare programs which would be eliminated by the negative income tax relates to the need for "pride swallowing." To gain assistance from existing income support programs, the poor must submit to detailed and regular investigations by welfare workers checking on indigence and the characteristics necessary for eligibility. Some observers have noted that many poor families are not now receiving welfare assistance because of these degrading and demoralizing practices. The negative income tax, because it is universal and an integral part of the regular personal income tax structure, would avoid the social stigma of existing welfare programs.

A final characteristic of the existing welfare system which would be eliminated by the negative income tax is the "100 percent tax rate" currently applied to many welfare recipients. Under many existing programs, the income assistance given the poor person is reduced $1 for every $1 which he earns by working. The poor person, in effect, faces a 100 percent tax rate. Because he experiences no increase in his income if he seeks a job, he is given substantial incentive *not* to work.[9] The negative income tax would avoid this situation through a structure of rates which would permit the poor person to keep (at least) some of any income which he might earn. This incentive-to-work arrangement would be a significant improvement over existing welfare practices.

The basic mechanics of the negative income tax are identical to those of the existing, positive, income tax. The existing tax *takes* a certain amount of the income earned by a person *if* he earns more than a specified income level; the negative income tax would *give* a certain amount of income to a person *if* he fails to

[8] It should be noted that to the extent that the negative income tax is simply substituted for these other programs, it may fail to reduce the poverty gap.
[9] That is, unless he can earn more on the job than his *total* assistance payment.

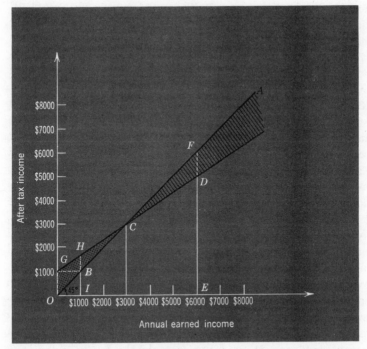

Figure 10-1

attain a specified income level. This distinction can be seen in Figure 10-1.

On the horizontal axis of Figure 10-1 the amount of income earned by, say, a family of four is plotted. The vertical axis measures how much income the family has left after it pays its income tax; that is, after-tax income. Clearly, if there were no income tax, the family's before-tax income (horizontal axis) would equal its after-tax income (vertical axis). With no income tax, then, the relationship between the family's before-tax and after-tax incomes is given by the 45° line, *OBCFA*.

First, let us show the effect of the current, positive income tax structure. For a family of four with standard deductions, no tax is paid on income below $3000. Below $3000 of annual income, after-tax and before-tax incomes are equal. However, earned, taxable income above that level is taxed at the rates shown in Table 6-1. With the existing income tax structure, then, the relationship between after-tax and before-tax income is given by the kinked curve *OBCD*—the income tax paid increases as income increases, but only after $3000. Consequently, given any before-tax income (and certain assumptions about exemptions and deductions), after-tax income can be read on the vertical axis from *OBCD*. For example, a before-tax income to a family of four of $6000 (*OE* = *EF*) would produce an after-tax income of *ED* with *DF* being paid in income taxes. In the diagram, the shaded area represents the "tax bite." While the positive tax structure will not take any money from a family of four with less than $3000 of income, neither will it provide assistance to that family. As long as the tax is a positive tax, the after-tax–before-tax relationship will always lie *on* or *below* the 45° line.[10]

The negative income tax structure is the converse of the positive income tax—it gives direct payments to a family if their earned income fails to attain a certain level. This is shown in Figure 10-1 by the after-tax–before-tax curve *GHC* which applies to low income groups. This curve lies above the 45° line. A family of four which earns below $3000 would not only pay no taxes; it would receive a direct income payment if there were a negative income tax. The after-tax income of the family would be *greater* than its before-tax income. For example, the family of four with a before-tax income of $1000 (*OI* = *IB*), would end up with an after-tax income of *IH*. An allowance of *BH* is granted to supplement the $1000 of earned income. The dotted area, therefore, represents the allowances granted to families which earn income of less than the specified level. If a tax structure had both positive and negative tax rates, its before-tax–after-tax curve might look like *GHCD*, lying above the 45° line at low incomes, below the 45° line at high incomes, and intersecting the 45° line at the income level at which the tax structure changes from negative to positive taxation.

As might be anticipated, a number of schemes have been proposed to combine both negative and positive taxation in a single tax structure. Figure 10-2 and Table 10-2 present some of the primary characteristics of two of these proposals. The first of these

[10] In a certain sense, the existing, positive tax structure discriminates against the very poor—the family without any income and the family with $3000 of income are both given tax-free status.

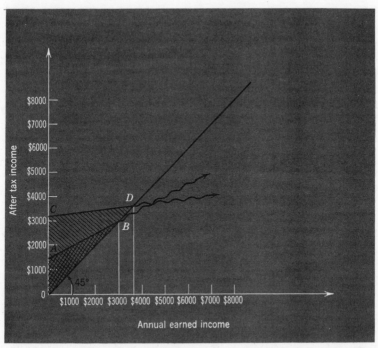

Figure 10-2

plans has been suggested by Milton Friedman, an economist at
the University of Chicago, whom we quoted at length in Chapter
1. According to Friedman's plan, all families would file an income
tax return, the first step of which is to calculate the value of ex-

Table 10-2. Two Negative Income Tax Schemes, Family of Four

	Friedman Plan		Theobald Plan	
Earned Income	After-Tax Income	Amount of Allowance	After-Tax Income	Amount of Allowance
$ 0	$1500	$1500	$3200	$3200
500	1750	1250	3250	2750
1000	2000	1000	3300	2300
1500	2250	750	3350	1850
2000	2500	500	3400	1400
2500	2750	250	3450	950
3000	3000	0	3500	500
3500	less than 3500	0	3550	50
4000	less than 4000	0	less than 4000	0

emptions and deductions. For our standard family of four, for example, exemptions are $2400 (4 × $600) and deductions are $600, for a total of $3000. This figure becomes the benchmark to which earned income is compared. If the family's earned income is below $3000 (say, $1200), the difference between these two values would be calculated ($1800) and a "tax rate" of 50 percent would be applied. The resulting figure is the amount which the low-income family would be paid by the government. In our example, this figure is $900 ($1800 × .5), providing the family with an after-tax income of $2100 ($1200 + $900). Friedman describes his plan as follows.

The advantages of this arrangement are clear! It is directed specifically at the problem of poverty. It gives help in the form most useful to the individual, namely, cash. It is general and could be substituted for the host of special measures now in effect. It makes explicit the cost borne by society. It operates outside the market. Like any other measures to alleviate poverty, it reduces the incentives of those helped to help themselves, but it does not eliminate that incentive entirely, as a system of supplementing incomes up to some fixed minimum would. An extra dollar earned always means more money available for expenditure.[11]

The second plan has been proposed by Robert Theobald in his book *Free Markets and Free Men*.[12] The calculations for this plan are even easier than for Friedman's. Theobald accepts as his benchmark the federal government's estimate of the poverty line. Presumably, this cut-off line for a family of four would be about $3200.[13] Theobald would guarantee each family of four a minimum of this benchmark and, in addition, would allow them to keep 10 percent of any income which they might earn while receiving a government negative tax allowance. For example, a family of four with $1200 of earned income would have an after-tax income of $3200 plus 10 percent of $1200 for a total of $3320.

[11] Milton Friedman, *Capitalism and Freedom* (Chicago: University of Chicago Press, 1962), p. 192. (Reprinted with permission).
[12] (New York: C. N. Potter Co., 1963).
[13] At the time both Friedman and Theobald were writing, the poverty cut-off line for a family of four was placed at about $3200. Recently, because of inflation and other factors, the cut-off line has been raised to about $3500. In our discussion of the mechanics of these negative income tax plans, we are using the $3200 cut-off figure.

The payment from the government would, therefore, be $2120 [$3200 − (.9 × $1200)].

In Figure 10-2, the before-tax–after-tax relationship is *AB* for Friedman's plan and *CD* for Theobald's. Both Figure 10-2 and Table 10-2 demonstrate that Theobald's plan provides a much higher income guarantee for the family living in poverty than does Friedman's. Indeed, Theobald's plan is a "poverty eliminating" scheme, whereas Friedman's only reduces the level of poverty. As can be seen from Table 10-2, a family with no income is granted an allowance of only $1500 in Friedman's plan, leaving a poverty gap of $1700; Theobald's scheme eliminates poverty. Obviously, the dollar cost of the two plans to the federal government reflects the differences in the level of income guarantee. It is estimated that the implementation of Friedman's plan would cost under $10 billion a year; Theobald's scheme is projected to cost upwards of $25 billion annually.[14]

These two proposals have other significant differences which should also be noted. First, the Friedman plan reflects a significant concern with providing incentives to work. It is designed to encourage the low income worker to expend productive effort by permitting him to keep 50 percent of every dollar that he earns. This is a significant increase in work incentive as compared to the 100 percent tax rate which is implied by many existing welfare programs. The Theobald plan shows far less concern with work incentives. A poor family is only allowed to keep 10¢ out of every additional dollar it earns; this is equivalent to a 90 percent tax rate. Second, because of its relatively high minimum income guarantee, the Theobald plan provides some subsidy support to people *above* the poverty line; Friedman's does not. This is seen both in Figure 10-2 and in Table 10-2. With Theobald's plan, a family which earned income of $3500 would still be granted an

[14] While the dollar cost of these programs is rather large, it must be emphasized that their real cost is only a fraction of their budgetary cost. This is so because the negative income tax is, basically, an income transfer scheme. It redistributes income from the rich to the poor with no necessary effect on the nation's real income. However, in evaluating these proposals, one must not neglect the fact that they may have some impact on the volume of goods and services produced by the economy. This impact would occur if the scheme affects the abilities and desires of citizens to work and invest. (See the discussion in Chapter 5.)

allowance. In Friedman's scheme, a family with this income level would be paying taxes. Finally, Friedman offers his plan as a substitute for many existing income assistance programs. He argues that if his proposal is adopted, social security, medicare, old age assistance, public health assistance, and so on *should* be reduced or eliminated.[15] On the other hand, while Theobald's scheme would eliminate the need for many existing welfare and assistance programs, he advocates the continuance (indeed, extension) of a wide range of social service programs, including medical care.

While the negative income tax has a good deal to commend it, especially as it compares to existing welfare programs, it has some basic problems which make it, as yet, unacceptable politically. In addition to its cost in terms of budgetary resources, there is the bothersome problem of work incentives. Even the relatively modest Friedman scheme entails a marginal tax rate of 50 percent, which is among the highest tax rates in the positive income tax structure. While no one knows the relationship between marginal incomes and incentives, many are concerned about a potential adverse impact on national productivity due to the implementation of such a plan. Currently, an experiment is being conducted on a sample of low income people to determine the effect of different tax rates on their willingness to work. The results of this research should shed light on the seriousness of this work incentive problem.

Another unresolved problem with negative income tax proposals relates to administration and enforcement. There is some concern that, without the controls of the existing welfare system, a tax system with negative rates would encourage widespread misreporting of incomes. While most experts regard this problem to be both complex and technical, they are optimistic that it can be solved.

C. *The Family Assistance System—*
A Nixon Administration Proposal

In August 1969, at the height of discussions on strategies for assisting the poor, the Nixon Administration submitted its plan

[15] It should be noted that the savings from eliminating these programs should be subtracted from the cost of Friedman's negative income tax scheme.

for reform of the welfare system and financial assistance to low income families. Clearly, this proposal was designed to be the Republican alternative to negative income tax and guaranteed annual income schemes.

The primary characteristics of the Family Assistance System are as follows.

1. It would be related to the nation's existing welfare system but would represent a major overhaul of much of the current system. This is to be contrasted to the negative income tax which bears no necessary relationship to the existing system.

2. Through the system, a nationwide basic welfare minimum would be established and applied to all states. This minimum would be $1600 per year for a family of four; about 50 percent of the poverty cut-off level. Such a federally established minimum, however, would raise the benefit level of the 20 lowest states which now provide basic welfare payments of less than that figure.

3. The basic allowance of $1600 for the low income family would be reduced as the family's private (or earned) income increased, but some percentage of any earned income could be retained. In fact, 100 percent of the first $720 of earned income could be retained without a reduction in the basic $1600 allowance. In effect, then, a family of four could secure $2320 of income ($1600 + $720) before increments to income would be eroded by diminished benefits. After the first $720 of earnings, the low income family would be allowed to keep 50¢ of each additional dollar earned. All federal assistance would stop when earned income equaled $3920. Table 10-3 summarizes the payment schedule for the Nixon scheme. The numbers in it are directly comparable with those for the Friedman and Theobald plans shown in Table 10-2.

From the comparison, it is seen that the Family Assistance System is more generous than the Friedman proposal in that it provides a higher basic allowance—$1600 as compared to $1500— and enables the low income family to retain 100 percent of its first $720 of earned income. However, after the first $720, the decrease in allowance as earned income increases occurs at the same 50 percent rate as in the Friedman plan.

Relative to the Theobald plan, the Nixon scheme is a parsimo-

Table 10-3. The Family Assistance System, Family of Four

Earned Income	After-Tax Income	Amount of Allowance
$ 0	$1600	$1600
720	2320	1600
1000	2460	1460
2000	2960	960
3000	3460	460
3920	3920	0

nious one. This is seen by comparing the total income levels for the very poorest families. While Theobald would eliminate the poverty gap, the Nixon scheme leaves a significant income gap for the very poorest people.

4. As a means of getting able-bodied citizens "onto payrolls" and "off welfare rolls," the Family Assistance System would require all heads of families (except mothers of preschool children or those physically or mentally unable to work) participating in the program to register with a local employment service. If a "suitable" job or job training vacancy became available, the participant would be obliged to accept it. If he refused to work in the available job or if he refused to enter the training program, the family would lose a portion of its basic allowance.

5. In order to accommodate the substantial increase in the demand for job-training slots generated by the system, the Nixon proposal included a substantial increase in federally sponsored vocational education programs. Similarly, there would be a substantial increase in the funding of day care centers to encourage mothers of dependent children to seek work or training.

Except for the fact that the Family Assistance program works through the welfare (or direct payment) system rather than the income tax structure, it is clear that it bears close resemblance to negative income tax proposals. Like these proposals, it eliminates many of the undesirable characteristics of the existing welfare system: it provides a basic nationwide system of income support; it incorporates a positive work incentive; it gives support to a family with an able-bodied father who is unemployed and unable to find work. However, because it is part of the welfare system, it fails to overcome many of the degrading and demoralizing characteristics of that system. As mentioned earlier, a serious problem of the welfare system involves the procedures, checks, and investigations undertaken by welfare agencies to determine the eligibility of a family for assistance.

II. TAX EXPENDITURES AND TAX CREDITS

We have seen that the taxing-spending process shifts and reallocates an enormous volume of the society's resources. The revenue or tax side of the budget records the government's withdrawal of funds from the private sector, causing consumers and businesses to purchase fewer goods and services than they otherwise would. The expenditure side of the account records the government's use of the funds withdrawn. A large proportion of these funds—the direct expenditures—are used to purchase goods and services from the private sector. The effect of this withdrawal and direct spending is to shift the allocation of the nation's labor and capital from the production of goods purchased by private citizens to the production of goods purchased by the government.

Assuming that the federal budget must be roughly balanced over the period of, say, the next decade, it follows that there are two ways in which the taxing-spending process can be used to alter the flow of society's resources. First, government spending can be increased or decreased and, when matched by taxes, can directly reallocate resources from private to public uses. Second, special allowances, exemptions, deductions, or credits can be inserted into the tax law to provide preferential treatment to some activity or to somebody. As we discussed in Chapter 7, these special provisions grant tax advantages to people for doing certain things or having certain kinds of income. By providing additional income to certain people, they shift resources in the same way that direct government spending entails resource reallocation. In both cases, the allocation of resources is modified because of a conscious public decision. Because of this symmetrical effect, these special tax provisions have been called "tax expenditures." Some have called them "backdoor spending."

As an example of a tax expenditure, consider the special tax privileges granted to natural resource industries, in the form of the depletion allowances and other special provisions. While the federal budget shows direct expenditures of about $2 billion for natural resource development objectives, it fails to show another $1.7 billion of assistance in the form of these special tax provisions or tax expenditures granted to natural resource industries. This $1.7 billion represents taxes that were *not* paid because of some special tax provision. The case of assistance to the aged is another example. While the budget of the Department of Health, Education, and Welfare shows substantial expenditures for assistance to older people, it fails to show the $2.3 billion "expended through the tax system to aid older people."[16]

Until recently, little has been known about the size and composition of tax expenditures. Unlike government spending:

> our Federal budget . . . does not report those tax revenues which the government does not collect because [the tax base] is reduced by . . . special provisions . . . , special credits, deductions, exclusions, and exemptions. . . .[17]

Because the budget fails to account for tax expenditures, the importance of this means of reallocating social resources has not been recognized. Nor has it been possible to evaluate the extent to which the "programs" implicit in these tax expenditures are attaining the government's objectives.

Within the last few years, however, the U.S. Treasury Department has attempted to document the tax expenditure problem. Analysts in the Treasury have studied the federal tax structure and have estimated the amount of tax revenue which the government "loses"—fails to collect—because of these special tax provisions and privileges. To relate these lost revenues or tax expenditures to direct federal spending, this Treasury study allocated tax expenditures among the functional expenditure categories used in the federal budget. In adopting this procedure, the Treasury stated:

[16] These tax expenditures include the special $600 exemption for people over 65 in the personal income tax, the retirement income credit, and the exclusion of social security benefits. See U.S. Congress, Joint Economic Committee, *Hearings on the Economic Report of the President, 1969*, testimony of Joseph Barr, Secretary of the Treasury, Jan. 17, 1969, pp. 11 ff.

[17] U.S. Treasury Department, *Annual Report of the Secretary of the Treasury*, 1968, p. 326.

Table 10-4. Federal Government Direct Expenditures and Tax Expenditures, Fiscal Year 1970 ($ Billions)

Budget Functions	Direct Expenditures	Tax Expenditures	Tax Expenditures as a Percent of Direct Expenditures
National defense	$81.5	$ .6	1
International affairs	3.7	.5	14
Space programs	3.9	0	0
Agriculture	5.2	1.0	19
Natural resources	1.9	1.7	90
Commerce and transportation	9.0	9.7	108
Housing and community development	2.8	5.2	186
Health and welfare	55.0	19.5	36
Education and manpower	7.9	.9	11
Veterans benefits	7.8	.7	9
Interest	16.0	0	0
General government	3.3	0	0
Aid to state and local governments	N.A.[a]	4.6	N.A.[a]
(Capital gains)[b]	N.A.[a]	5.5–8.5	N.A.[a]

Source. U.S. Congress, Joint Economic Committee, *Hearings on the Economic Report of the President, 1969, op. cit.,* pp. 11 ff.

[a] Not applicable since this is not a budget category.

[b] Capital gains are clearly tax expenditures. They are not allocable to any single functional category, however.

Since these tax expenditures serve ends similar to those which are . . . served by direct expenditure programs . . . , it would be appropriate and instructive to juxtapose the tax provisions and the revenue costs they involve with the [direct] expenditures in the same functional category in order to understand better the purpose to which public resources are allocated.[18]

In Table 10-4, the results of this calculation are shown for FY 1970. There it is seen that tax expenditures account for a major

[18] *Ibid.,* p. 329.

portion of the total impact of the budget on the allocation of the nation's resources. While in some categories nearly all of the budget's effect is through direct expenditures, there are a number of functional areas in which tax expenditures play a significant, indeed dominant, role. In fact, in both the commerce and transportation and the housing and community development areas, tax expenditures *exceed* direct budget outlays. In total, tax expenditures represent about $50 billion of budget resources—approximately one-fourth the amount of direct expenditures.

Tax expenditures have gained prominence in recent policy discussions for two primary reasons. First, it is becoming increasingly recognized that the application of economic analysis to public expenditures cannot stop with only the evaluation of direct outlays. Because many tax expenditures have economic impacts similar (or contrary) to existing direct expenditure programs, comprehensive policy analysis requires that both modes of expending budget resources be evaluated.

The past failure to recognize tax expenditures as having economic impacts similar to direct spending was evident in the recent Congressional debate over legislation to control federal expenditures. In the debate, no real recognition was given the fact that eliminating tax expenditures would have the same effect as reducing direct expenditures. Similarly, when the Bureau of the Budget implemented the expenditure control legislation, tax expenditures were excluded from their scrutiny because they were not explicit budget items. Because these hidden tax expenditures have not been carefully scrutinized, some of the most economically inefficient public programs have gone unnoticed by both policymakers and analysts. Former Assistant Secretary of the Treasury Stanley Surrey has put it this way:

I cannot think of any responsible HEW or Budget Bureau officials who would put together an expenditure program of assistance to the elderly that would in any way resemble the crazy-quilt pattern of our tax treatment of the elderly. Under that treatment half of the tax revenues spent go to people over age 65 on retirement whose annual income is over $10,000 and hardly any goes to people in that age group who continue to work for their maintenance and whose incomes are far lower. Nor can I think of an agricultural expert who would put together a farm program under which the benefits would become greater the wealthier the owner and the less he relied on his farm activity as the source of his income. Indeed, I suspect that cost-benefit experts assigned to measure the efficiency of tax expenditure programs would have a fascinating time. Appropriate budgetary recognition of these tax expenditures would facilitate such cost-benefit studies.[19]

A second reason for the current prominence of the tax expenditure issue relates to the discussion of strategies for solving problems of poverty and the ghetto. It will be recalled that the Nixon Administration took office with the pledge to seek solutions to these problems by providing financial assistance through the tax system. The mechanism which was most discussed in the 1968 Presidential campaign was that of the *tax credit*. Through this technique, businesses would be allowed to subtract a certain percentage of their expenditures for specified social service functions from their tax bill. Among the functions suggested as being legitimate objects of support through tax credits were job-training programs and the location of plants in urban ghetto and low-income rural areas. During the campaign, President Nixon stated:

I urge enactment by Congress of legislation providing tax incentives to corporations which hire and train the unskilled and upgrade the skills of those at the bottom of the employment ladder. A few years ago, American industry was given a seven percent tax credit for the modernization of equipment. The credits were widely used. Productivity increased, and the entire economy benefited. A similar tax credit for increasing the productivity of people is overdue.[20]

As President Nixon's remarks imply, recent proposals to use tax credits to achieve social objectives are modeled on the Investment Tax Credit which we discussed in Chapter 7. By permitting businesses to pay less taxes if they undertake investment spending, the investment tax credit subsidizes private industry for doing something which they would not have done on their own.

---

[19] *Ibid.*, p. 324. See also the testimony of Stanley Surrey in U.S. Congress, Joint Economic Committee, Subcommittee on Economy in Government, *Economic Analysis and the Efficiency of Government*, Hearings, 1970.

[20] Nixon-Agnew Campaign Committee, *Nixon on the Issues*, p. 113. In addition to these corporate tax credits, the granting of personal income tax credits to assist parents of college students in their purchase of higher education has long been discussed.

Through a "tax incentive," private business is induced to undertake activities which satisfy social objectives.

In the recent discussion of tax credits, a number of pro and con arguments have been made concerning this form of tax expenditure. Those who oppose using the tax credit to achieve social objectives argue that it is a terribly blunt instrument. They point out that if tax credits are built into the tax laws, some businesses will be subsidized for doing what they would have done without the subsidy—the tax credit will be pure profit to them. For example, many businesses now undertake job training as a regular part of their hiring policy. Would they be able to deduct this normal business expense directly from their taxes if tax credit legislation is passed?

Opponents of tax credit legislation also note that the government will have very little control over the kinds of social development programs which are induced by the tax incentive. For example, would job-training programs emphasize those skills which the economy most needs? Perhaps the skills which would be generated by programs induced by tax credits are those already in excess supply. Moreover, because the programs would be "tax supported," the Internal Revenue Service would be required to play a coordinating role. It is the only agency with responsibility to administer the tax law. Personnel in this agency are clearly not equipped to deal with these complex social problems.

Those who oppose these schemes also point out that special provisions which get built into the tax law are terribly difficult to remove. In part this is due to the political pressure of those who are receiving subsidies from the special provision. Because the social problems to which these new schemes are addressed are, hopefully, not permanent ones, it is worrisome to contemplate these special provisions built into the semi-permanent tax law. Former Assistant Secretary of the Treasury Surrey has stated:

Our experience with the tax incentives of the past should give us pause before we add a new tax-route expenditure and then keep it buried in the Code away from public scrutiny. We have learned that the tax incentive of the moment becomes the tax reform target of many tomorrows.[21]

21 U.S. Treasury Department, *op. cit.*, p. 325.

Those who support tax credits as a means of solving social and urban problems are not without arguments of their own. While they recognize that tax credits will reduce current federal tax revenue, they argue that the new programs will create productive citizens and regions where there was once unemployment and depression. Over the long run, they argue, this increased productivity will add to the tax base of the nation and will result in increased federal revenues.[22]

Advocates of tax credits also argue that the cost to the government of new social programs will be less through "tax expenditures" than through direct outlays. This is so because with tax credits, the government may not have to bear the full cost of programs. By providing an incentive, it draws private resources into these activities; it provides "seed capital." President Nixon stated this case for tax credits as follows.

[Tax credits] use and strengthen private institutions, rather than replacing them with public bureaucracies. They disperse administrative responsibilities to lower and more local levels rather than overcentralizing them. They allow for more variety, flexibility and experimentation rather than perpetuating over-rigid federal directives. They bring out private investment funds to help get the job done. I like a mix of incentives and direct expenditures, but the balance must be corrected in favor of more incentives.[23]

The question of using special tax provisions to achieve social objectives rather than direct expenditures is, therefore, an open and much-debated question. The need for having information on tax expenditures displayed on a regular basis and in the same categories as direct expenditures is less controversial. Nearly all would agree that such explicit information openly displayed is a necessary ingredient in the formation of consistent and effective public policy.

III. NATIONAL PRIORITIES AND MILITARY SPENDING

In recent years, the federal budget has become increasingly used as a means for attaining national objectives. When President

---

[22] It should be noted that direct expenditures to attack these problems will, over time, have the same effect on federal tax revenue.

[23] Nixon-Agnew Campaign Committee, *op. cit.*, p. 133.

Kennedy declared that placing a man on the moon was of high national priority, it was the federal budget, through expenditures on the space program, which was used to attain the objective. When President Johnson declared his War on Poverty, it was the items in the social assistance and human resource development portions of the budget which showed the most rapid increases.

Today the question of national priorities is a subject of wide concern. A sense of the national problems, each of which demands resources for its solution, is conveyed by each day's news. There is the urban crisis with its sub-crises of traffic congestion, air pollution, inadequate housing, unemployment, discrimination, and ghetto poverty; there is the "crisis" in higher education, with colleges and universities claiming insufficient financing to maintain quality education; there is the rural poverty problem with certain regions of the country becoming stagnant while the rest of the country develops rapidly; there is the problem of inadequate health services, with both doctor and hospital facilities in short supply; there is the environmental pollution problem and the problem of crime, violence, and delinquency. All of these are serious, and the solution of each will require large public expenditures. It is the federal budget which will undoubtedly bear the brunt of the enormous demands which these problems imply —either through direct or tax expenditures.

The anticipated cessation of Vietnam hostilities has again focused attention on the relationship between national problems requiring public action and the federal budget. Citizens interested in finding solutions to each of these problems argue that the funds released from fighting in Vietnam ought to be diverted to those programs in which they are most interested.

A recent study by former Director of the Bureau of the Budget Charles L. Schultze has spotlighted this national priority– federal budget relationship.[24] Because of decisions already made, Schultze points out, certain parts of the federal budget are going to rise automatically over the next few years. Similarly, because the economy is likely to continue to grow, tax revenues will continue to rise (even with no change in tax rates or structure). It

[24] Charles L. Schultze, "Budget Alternatives After Vietnam," in Kermit Gordon, ed., *Agenda for the Nation* (Washington: The Brookings Institution, 1969).

is the *difference* between these two "automatically" increasing flows which will determine the volume of budgetary resources that the federal government will have available to devote to new high priority programs. This difference between unavoidable expenditures and automatically generated tax revenues Schultze calls the *fiscal dividend*. "It measures the budgetary resources which will become available without explicit policy decisions."

Using reasonable assumptions about the economy's growth, the timing of the cessation of the Vietnam War, and price increases, Dr. Schultze has estimated the size of the fiscal dividend from 1969 to 1974. Table 10-5 is based on his calculations. From these

Table 10-5. Projection of the Post-Vietnam War Fiscal Dividend, 1969–1974 ($ Billions)

Budget Item	1969	1971	1974
Federal revenues	$172	$203	$259
Federal expenditures	185	195	221
Civilian	107	126	147
Military	79	91	100
Less Vietnam savings	−1	−22	−26
Fiscal dividend	—	8	38

Source. Charles L. Schultze, "Budget Alternatives After Vietnam," in Kermit Gordon, ed., *Agenda for a Nation* (Washington, D.C.: The Brookings Institution), p. 19.

estimates, it is clear that, even with the phasing out of the Vietnam War, there will not be a great dividend of "free" budgetary resources which can be used to solve severe national problems and achieve other social objectives. Dr. Schultze estimates that by 1971 there will only be a modest fiscal dividend of $8 billion (out of a total federal budget of over $200 billion) which can be allocated to other programs. By 1974, assuming no new programs are started, the fiscal dividend will grow to $38 billion. This scenario is not an optimistic one. Clearly, the nation will not be able to rely on the natural evolution of the federal budget if it decides to substantially increase the resources allocated to the solution of pressing social problems or other unmet national needs.[25]

[25] It should be noted that cutting Federal taxes may be one of the unmet national needs to which the fiscal dividend could be devoted.

In spite of this pessimistic picture, there is no economic reason why the nation cannot free more resources for budgetary items of high national priority if it so chooses. Two possible means of securing additional "budgetary freedom" are immediately obvious: a further increase in taxes or a reduction in other public programs. While the issues involved in this choice are complex and impossible to discuss in any detail here, there is one recently expressed point of view which bears mightily on the size of the fiscal dividend and the volume of free budgetary resources.

In a recent paper, Carl Kaysen, who was a special assistant to President Kennedy on national security matters, argues that changed relationships in international affairs and revolutionary changes in military technology require the United States to reappraise its national defense strategy.[26] Instead of seeking security through increased military strength and the commitment to military superiority in all of its aspects, Dr. Kaysen argues that U.S. policy should strive for national security through restrictions in armaments and intensified efforts in seeking arms-control arrangements with other national powers. He states:

In plain words, the course of arms limitation, restrictions in deployment, and arms control is not only cheaper than that of continuing competition in arms and military confrontation; it is safer.[27]

On the basis of his suggestions for a revised military strategy, Dr. Kaysen projects the Pentagon budget after the Vietnam War ends. With a modified military posture, Dr. Kaysen argues that the military budget could be significantly reduced. Indeed, the defense budget which he proposes for 1974 is about $16 billion lower than Schultze's projection. With such cost and budgetary constraints imposed on military planners, about $16 billion could be added to the nation's fiscal dividend. This sort of reduction would require a rigorous screening of large and expensive weapons systems which have already been scheduled for production by the Pentagon, as well as other large items in the defense budget.[28]

---

[26] Carl Kaysen, "Military Strategy, Military Force, and Arms Control," in Kermit Gordon, ed., *Agenda for the Nation, op. cit.*
[27] *Ibid.*, p. 549.
[28] Among these weapons systems now under development are the Safeguard

Dr. Kaysen's analysis leaves one more optimistic concerning the potential size of the fiscal dividend and the ability of the federal government either to pursue additional social objectives or to reduce taxes. It must be emphasized, however, that there are significant pressures which may result in an expanded military budget rather than a smaller one. First, it has been pointed out that if the United States, consistent with its current military strategy, begins the development of new weapons systems, the Soviet Union will feel that it must also expand its military power—and the arms race will again be on. The increased level of uncertainty which occurs when such a dynamic process is taking place could lead to massive increases in the U.S. military budget. This factor has led Dr. Schultze to note:

Either decisions will be made to reduce [military] . . . expenditures [from levels implied by current strategy], or they may themselves create a situation in which further expenditure increases will occur. To the extent that this evaluation is correct, the post-Vietnam fiscal dividend will either be significantly increased by policies that reduce military spending or it will be significantly eroded by further additions to that spending. There may be no intermediate position.[29]

---

antiballistic missile system (at a minimum total cost of $7 to $10 billion), the Minuteman III missile (at a total cost of $4.6 billion), the Poseidon missile (at a total cost of $2.5 billion), four nuclear-powered aircraft carriers (at a total cost of $2.21 billion), new fast-attack submarines, a new carrier-based fighter aircraft, a new land-based fighter aircraft, and a new class of manned bomber. It should be noted that Schultze's estimate of the military budget is also a conservative one in that it assumes that expenditures for these weapons systems will only take place as expenditures on existing systems are phased out.

Two recent analyses have argued that between $9 and $11 billion could be cut from the defense budget "while retaining or even improving the current level of the nation's defense." See *Congressional Quarterly*, June 28, 1965, p. 1605, and Robert Benson, "How the Pentagon Can Save $9,000,-000,000," *Washington Monthly*, March 1969.

[29] Schultze, *op. cit.*, p. 42. It is interesting, and discouraging, to note that the Pentagon has projected that military spending *after* Vietnam will not be significantly reduced from the 1969 level of spending which included nearly $30 billion of Vietnam expenditures. See testimony of Robert C. Moot, Assistant Secretary of Defense, Comptroller, in U.S. Congress, Joint Economic Committee, Subcommittee on Economy in Government, *The Military Budget and National Economic Priorities*, Hearings, 1969.

Second, an increasing number of observers have noted the upward pressure placed on the military budget by the interlocking relationship of military men, political representatives from districts with large military installations, firms in the defense industries, and the community of scientists and analysts working on military or weapons research. It is argued that each member of this interlocking relationship—often referred to as the "military-industrial-scientific complex"—finds increased military spending to be in his own personal interest. Therefore, each adopts a strategy which will result in higher military spending. The recent request of the Joint Chiefs of Staff for a military budget in excess of $100 billion is not inconsistent with these pressures and does little to allay fears of their existence.

Finally, the uncertainties involved in producing new weapons systems, the lack of competition in the bidding for weapons contracts, and the failure of the Defense Department to develop effective incentive contracts, cost control, and performance measurement devices makes it likely that the actual costs of new weapons systems will be significantly greater than the Pentagon is now telling the Congress and the nation. The influence of these cost understatements on the military budget has been pinpointed recently by the investigation of the Congressional Joint Economic Committee into the contract between the Defense Department and the Lockheed Corporation for the production of the C-5A transport aircraft.[30] When the contract was signed, it was anticipated that the production of these huge military cargo planes would cost about $2.9 billion. The actual cost, however, will run to over $5 billion. It is not unusual for weapons systems to cost two to three times as much as the original contract stipulated.[31]

[30] U.S. Congress, Joint Economic Committee, Subcommittee on Economy in Government, *Economics of Military Procurement,* Hearings, 1969.
[31] The Joint Economic Committee in its 1969 Economic Report, stated: "We have been impressed by the evidence of widespread waste, mismanagement, and inefficiency in defense spending brought to light in recent months. It now seems clear that the present level of national security can be maintained on a substantially smaller defense budget. Much of the inefficiency, it appears, is found in defense procurement. While over $44 billion was spent on the purchase of weapons and other military goods last year, only 11 percent of the contracts were awarded through formal advertising. Sole source procurement accounts for 57.9 percent. It is in the sole source pro-

This factor also serves to boost the military budget above expectations. Its recognition requires still less optimism regarding the future size of the available fiscal dividend, that is, unless military spending comes under far more careful scrutiny and far more control by the Congress than it has in past years.

In addition to military expenditures, there are several other public expenditure programs which require careful screening. A number of these programs may have been high-priority items in past decades, but have since been superceded by more pressing needs. Among those which have often been cited as both inefficient and of low priority are the farm price-support programs, portions of the space program, the federal maritime program which subsidizes the U.S. merchant marine, the Post Office, and public works projects. It has been estimated that rigorous screening of these programs could add from $2 to $4 billion to the fiscal dividend by 1974.[32]

What this section has emphasized, then, is that wise public policy requires a careful delineation of objectives and priorities and a sensitive evaluation of alternative means of attaining them. It has shown that no public objective is attained at zero cost— that a thin antiballistic missile system costs several million hospital beds, several million low-income housing units, several thousand new schools, or several years' delay in halting the pollution of the environment. It has been argued that effective public policy requires that all alternatives—from military spending to farm programs to poverty programs to tax cuts—be subjected to economic evaluation in light of explicit national objectives and the priority assigned to them.

curement of major weapons systems where much of the problem of excessive costs and cost overruns have occurred."

[32] See, for example, Charles L. Schultze, *op. cit.*, p. 47. See also U.S. Congress, Joint Economic Committee, Subcommittee on Economy in Government, *Economic Analysis and the Efficiency of Government*, Hearings and Report, 1970, for an appraisal of the inefficiency and inequity generated by a number of these traditional programs.

Index